"*Making Today Count for Eternity* tackles one of the most exciting, yet overlooked topics in Scripture. For years I have preached about the significance of our eternal reward and its relationship to life here on earth. At last someone has published a book that has the potential to serve as a wake-up call to the church. I agree with Kent Crockett when he writes, 'The few brief moments you live on earth will determine your responsibilities for all eternity.'"

ANDY STANLEY, SENIOR PASTOR
NORTH POINT COMMUNITY CHURCH,
ATLANTA, GEORGIA

"It's easy to get caught up in busy schedules and endless to-do lists, forgetting about what truly matters in life. Kent Crockett reminds us that our daily actions really can make a difference for eternity. In *Making Today Count for Eternity*, Kent pulls back the curtains and lets the refreshing glow of life break through."

TED HAGGARD, SENIOR PASTOR
NEW LIFE CHURCH,
COLORADO SPRINGS, COLORADO

"*Making Today Count for Eternity* encourages us to examine the meaning of life and fulfill our destinies. Kent Crockett has used his gift of writing to lift us above the fray of this fallen world to give us a higher view of God's eternal plan."

JIMMY EVANS, HOST OF FAMILY AND MARRIAGE
TODAY TELEVISION MINISTRY
SENIOR PASTOR, TRINITY FELLOWSHIP CHURCH,
AMARILLO, TEXAS

"Kent Crockett shows how to apply scriptural truth to everyday living while maintaining the simplicity of devotion to Jesus. If you will put into practice the advice in *Making Today Count for Eternity*, it will serve you well in your pursuit of God."

PETER LORD, BIBLE TEACHER AND AUTHOR,
TITUSVILLE, FLORIDA
AUTHOR OF
HEARING GOD AND KEEPING THE DOORS OPEN

MAKING TODAY COUNT FOR
ETERNITY

KENT CROCKETT

Multnomah®Publishers *Sisters, Oregon*

MAKING TODAY COUNT FOR ETERNITY
published by Multnomah Publishers, Inc.
and in association with the literary agency of Steven L. Green
© 2001 by Kent Crockett

International Standard Book Number: 1-57673-740-3

Cover image by Brad Wilson/Photonica

Scripture quotations are from:
New American Standard Bible © 1960, 1977, 1995
by the Lockman Foundation. Used by permission.

Also quoted:
The Holy Bible, King James Version (KJV)
The Holy Bible, New International Version (NIV)
© 1973, 1984 by International Bible Society,
used by permission of Zondervan Publishing House
Holy Bible, New Living Translation (NLT)
© 1996. Used by permission of Tyndale House Publishers, Inc.
All rights reserved.

Italics in Scripture have been added by the author for emphasis.

Multnomah is a trademark of Multnomah Publishers, Inc.,
and is registered in the U.S. Patent and Trademark Office.

The colophon is a trademark of Multnomah Publishers, Inc.
Printed in the United States of America

For information:
MULTNOMAH PUBLISHERS, INC. • P.O. BOX 1720 • SISTERS, OR 97759

Library of Congress Cataloging-in-Publication Data:

Crockett, Kent, 1952–
    Making today count for eternity / by Kent Crockett.
    p. cm.
ISBN 1-57673-740-3 (pbk.)
1. Heaven—Christianity. I. Title.
BT846.3.C76 2001
236'.2—dc21
                                    00-013151

01 02 03 04 05—10 9 8 7 6 5 4 3 2 1 0

To my wife, girlfriend, and best friend, Cindy.
You still make my heart beat faster.

ACKNOWLEDGMENTS

My thanks to the following:

My Lord, Jesus Christ, for preparing an eternal home for me. I know where I'd be without You.

My wife, Cindy, Matt Maxwell, Megg Rubbo, Cathy Evans, Brenda Howard, and Alesa Meschberger for critiquing my rough drafts.

My children, Hannah and Scott. You make me glad that I'm your father.

My friend Pat Howard. Thanks for all your help on the computer and Internet.

Paul and Debby Baskin. Cindy and I cherish our friendship with you.

Mike Luskey, Keith Sanderson, Don Hughes, and the entire staff at KJIL Christian radio station, Meade, Kansas. You encourage me more than you'll ever know.

Peter Lord. You have taught me much about the living God, my friend.

My brothers, Stuart and Bruce. I'm doubly blessed to have you as natural and spiritual brothers.

The members of Cornerstone Church. Thanks for all your love and support. It's a pleasure to see your smiling faces every Sunday.

My editor, Jeff Gerke. After transplanting chapters and performing surgery on sentences, the patient is doing well. Thanks, Doc.

My agent, Steven L. Green. God is using you in unique ways to further His kingdom. You are a blessing.

Don Jacobson and the Multnomah family. I'm honored that we could work together on this project.

Contents

Part 1: The Meaning of Our Earthly Existence

Part 2: A Glimpse into Eternity Future

Part 3: Preparing for the Next Life

Foreword

North of Houston, there lies a city by the name of Humble, Texas. Although it now boasts a large population, I remember the days when it was so small that only a caution light alerted people to it as they drove past. It was there that I attended junior and senior high school with Kent Crockett.

Even then Kent impressed me as a deep thinker. Today he is reaching people with both the spoken and written Word. Over the years I have enjoyed his ministry as well as his friendship.

Kent's latest book, *Making Today Count for Eternity*, continues the pattern of excellence I have come to expect from someone who is scholarly and yet very approachable. His marvelous insight, presented in a down-to-earth way, will both challenge and encourage the reader.

David Meece

A Word from the Author

Some of the Scriptures I examine in *Making Today Count for Eternity* could be interpreted as applying to Christ's millennial reign. My interpretation of eternity and God's future rewards is at times speculative. However, it is not unreasonable to assume that there is continuity between the Millennium and God's eternal kingdom. My purpose in writing this book is to focus on how our earthly lives will affect our eternal destinies, not to debate views on end times. If you would like to find out more about how you can make today count for eternity, log on to my web site at www.kentcrockett.com.

INTRODUCTION

The one who had once been called Jerry stood on the riverbank in awe.

Towering over him was the largest tree he had ever seen. In his moment on earth—those fifty-six years of life already mostly faded from his memory—he'd once made a trip to California to see the tallest tree in the world, a 350-foot redwood. This tree made that one look like a sapling. Jerry had to turn his head to see both sides of its enormous base, though he was standing fifty feet away from it.

The tree of life.

Pure water gushed through the center of the tree, roaring as it rushed out of the golden city into the green expanse. The ripples glistened as the river slowed into a peaceful current. Jerry had seen the clear waters of Grand Bahama Island, but that was mud runoff compared to this.

The river of life.

"Beautiful, isn't it?"

Jerry turned around. A woman sat on the grass behind him. She looked like she'd been there for some time. "Oh, sorry, I didn't see you. How long have you been sitting there?"

She shrugged. "Seven or eight thousand years, I guess? Maybe a billion. Nobody really keeps track of time anymore. No point, really."

"Yeah, I guess you're right."

Jerry tried not to stare at the letters shining on the woman's forehead. They were written in a language he'd never seen, but somehow he knew it was the name of Jesus Christ. He touched his own forehead and felt the delicate calligraphy there. Jerry shut his eyes and thought about the Name on his forehead. *Praise You, Lord, for making me free at last!*

"You're new here, aren't you?" she asked.

"Is it obvious?"

"Yes, but that's all right." With a sweep of her arm, she displayed the lush fields, the river, the tree, and the spires of the shining city. "This place has that effect on everyone. It's the first time any of us has seen perfection."

Jerry nodded, watching a group of swimmers jump, laughing, into the river of life.

"Where will you be working?" she asked.

"At the Northwest Gate of the City."

"Oh, that's quite an honor. You must've done well in your Opportunity."

"My what?"

"Your Opportunity," she said, smiling in the even glow of the day. "You know: your life—your time on earth."

"Oh. I guess I never really thought of it as an opportunity."

"Well, when else were you going to have the chance to determine what your position would be for eternity? You certainly can't do it once you get here."

Jerry blinked at her a few times. "You mean *that's* what my life was all about?"

"Sure. It was your Test. Your placement exam for all this. But let's not talk about that now. I want to show you something."

The woman led him toward the tree of life. Suddenly they were high in its branches. Jerry clutched a nearby limb, but the woman laughed. "You can't fall, you know. Jesus undid the Fall."

Jerry looked at her curiously.

"What, you thought we wouldn't have humor in heaven?" She winked at him and plucked a succulent-looking yellow fruit from the tree. "These are great." She took a bite and handed it to him. "November's fruit is my favorite. This is where I work—up here in the tree."

Jerry examined the fruit, thinking of another one plucked long ago.

"Don't worry about that," she said. "This fruit was never forbidden."

From his vantage point, Jerry scanned the massive wall surrounding the new Jerusalem, trying to pick out the shimmering gate where he would be working.

"You see that man up there?" the woman asked, pointing to another branch.

Jerry finally noticed that there were people in the tree with them—hundreds of people moving confidently about the branches, harvesting fruit and plucking leaves. "Which one?"

"The one with the basket. See him?"

"Oh, yeah. What about him?"

"He really did well in his Opportunity. Look at him. He's one of the chief gardeners supervising the care of the tree of life. You don't get that kind of job without doing something right in the Test."

"Wow," Jerry said, biting into the fruit, "was he a celebrity or president or something? No, what am I saying? I bet he was a missionary to Africa or India or Outer Mongolia. He was, wasn't he?"

She shook her head.

"Come on, give. How'd he do it? How'd he get that great job?"

"He was a night watchman at a warehouse."

Jerry almost slipped. "He *what?*"

"That's right. And he was an usher at his church. He visited the elderly in rest homes. And he coached peewee soccer."

"You mean God actually thought any of that was important?"

"He was a loving husband until his wife died, after fifty-two years of marriage."

Jerry waited to hear the real reason for his prominent assignment.

"And he was a giving father. He set a great example for his children and was always there for them."

He opened his hands. "And?"

"And what?"

"What else did he do? What are you hiding? He did something really big, didn't he? I bet he was martyred for his faith, right? Why are you looking at me like that?"

She patted him on the shoulder. "You want to know the most important thing he did? He loved Jesus with all his heart. Even though he didn't make any headlines on earth, Jesus smiled as He watched him cheerfully fulfill his purpose on earth—his Opportunity. Come on, I'll take you to the Northwest Gate so you can see what you'll be doing."

The one who had once been called Jerry took the woman's out-

14

stretched hand. "Well, okay, I guess." They perched on the limb of the tree of life. "What *will* I be doing?"

"Greeting people who made the most of their Opportunity."

DOWN TO EARTH

What will you be doing 5.6 million years from now? Don't you think that heaven would be just a little bit boring if we didn't have anything to do forever? Lots of people talk about going to heaven, but few give thought to what they will be doing for those millions of years. Seems to me that when we get to heaven, our first words shouldn't be, "Yippee, I made it. Now what?"

Doesn't God have more to say about heaven than the fact that the streets are gold and the gates are pearl? Does the Bible give us any information about what will occur in eternity? You might be surprised to find out how much God has revealed to us.

What I am going to share with you will revolutionize your understanding of why God placed you here on earth. God has an exciting plan mapped out for eternity future. He offers you the Opportunity, through your life on earth, to be part of that plan.

The Creator of the universe designed you with a special purpose in mind. He has wonderful things in store for you, both in this life and the next. Now open your heart, and let's find out what they are. Your life is about to change—forever.

part one

The Meaning of Our Earthly Existence

A mother asked her son why he always read the end of the book first.

The boy replied, "Mom, it's better that way. No matter how much trouble the hero gets into, I don't have to worry, because I know how it's going to end."

God has announced ahead of time how the book of this life will end. The Hero wins, the bad guy loses, and all who follow Jesus will live happily ever after.

Because we know how it will end, we can now begin.

What Makes God Smile?

What advantage does man have in
all his work which he does under the sun?

ECCLESIASTES 1:3

Seems like a dream, it happened so long ago. After graduating from seminary and working as a counselor, I felt called to start a new church in a rural area in Kansas. I drafted my wife, Cindy, to help me in this endeavor.

In those days, Cindy's schedule included being the mother of an industrious toddler and a baby, working part-time at a preschool, and serving as a pastor's wife to boot. Every day she rinsed out dirty cloth diapers in the toilet because we couldn't afford disposables. She cleaned house, prepared meals, counseled women in distress, and worked diligently at her job.

And wondered if God was pleased with her life.

One day after completing her daily duties, Cindy sighed and

said, "Sometimes I feel like I'm not doing anything for God."

I felt the same way. Every weekday morning I got up at 4 A.M. to work at my part-time job at UPS to supplement my income. As pastor of a congregation of fifty people, my salary was $800 per month. I couldn't feed my family on that. I had to moonlight just so we could survive. We shopped at garage sales, clipped coupons, and bought used furniture.

Our new church didn't own property or a building. Every Sunday for several years we had to set up metal folding chairs and equipment in a rented facility. Sometimes we weren't able to use the building, so we had to meet in a park. I secretly wondered if God approved of our seemingly ineffective ministry.

Was this why I had spent eight years in college and seminary? No one would have even thought of calling us successful. This wasn't the picture of dynamic ministry that I had read about so often in Christian books and magazines. If the truth were known, we felt like failures. No one knew our names, much less cared what we were doing. We didn't have one shred of evidence that we were doing anything to please God.

That was over fifteen years ago. Our kids are grown now. No more dirty diapers to change. Cindy and I don't work part-time jobs anymore. The church I pastor no longer has to meet in a rented facility. Our congregation now owns twenty-two acres of property and a debt-free church building. I'm writing books and have been interviewed on numerous radio stations around the country.

Is God smiling yet?

That raises a critical question. What makes God smile? Many people have a preconceived idea about who is on God's most favored list. Here is the presumed pecking order, starting with those most likely to gain God's approval.

Presumed Hierarchy of God-Pleasers

Missionaries to Africa (Big smile)
All other missionaries
Pastors of large churches
Pastors of medium-sized churches (Medium smile)
Pastors of small churches
Elders and deacons
Sunday school teachers
Successful businesspeople (Small smile)
People who work at secular jobs
Night watchmen, custodians, stay-at-home mothers (No smile)

If the above scenario is true, less than one percent of the world's population is pleasing God. Come on now—be honest. Don't you really believe that you must reach a certain level of success before God will start grinning? Don't you have a sneaking suspicion that God likes your work only if you do it inside a church building?

For some reason, most people believe that God smiles only if we are ministering in the church. Without a doubt, that is important. Every Christian should be involved in a local fellowship. But isn't raising a family on God's approval list? How about random acts of kindness? God's kingdom stretches beyond the church house doors. The fact is that every person on the above list has the same potential to please the God of heaven.

When Jesus was baptized, a voice from heaven said, "This is My beloved Son, *in whom I am well-pleased*" (Matthew 3:17). At that time, Jesus was thirty years old, and He hadn't performed a miracle, preached a sermon, or taught a Sunday school class. He had spent most of His life sweeping sawdust in a carpenter's shop. Despite His lack of ministry experience, His Father was pleased with His life.

Although Jesus hadn't performed a miracle, preached a sermon, or taught a Sunday school class, His Father was well pleased with His life.

Not just pleased—*well* pleased.

How could His Father give His approval if Jesus hadn't performed any ministerial duties? Apparently ministry isn't the determining factor when it comes to pleasing God. Being famous isn't the key to making God happy, either. Jesus wasn't a celebrity when He was baptized. And He certainly wasn't popular when He hung on that cross.

What makes God smile? He smiles when His children cheerfully do what He says. It might be sweeping sawdust or preaching to multitudes. It might be changing diapers or working a part-time job to support your family. Or it might be writing books and being interviewed on the radio. It just depends on what God wants you to do at the time. King Solomon wrote, "I have seen the task which God has given the sons of men with which to occupy themselves. He has made everything appropriate in its time" (Ecclesiastes 3:10–11).

When I look back on the early years of our ministry, I can say confidently that God was smiling. We were obedient to what He wanted us to do at that time. When Cindy changed dirty diapers, wiped runny noses, and spooned in Gerber's baby food, God gave her a thumbs-up. When I climbed out of bed at four o'clock in the morning to work a secular job to feed my family, He nodded with approval. And yes, He attended every one of our services when the congregation numbered only fifty. Jesus promised that He wouldn't miss it. "For where two or three have gathered together in My name, I am there in their midst" (Matthew 18:20). It doesn't take a large crowd to grab His attention—just two or three people.

Which is more important: fifty churches with ten thousand members or ten thousand churches with fifty members? Each church has its place in God's kingdom. Nevertheless, many pastors of small churches feel terribly unimportant. It's easy to feel insignificant when the spotlight never shines on you. But we've got to stop thinking that God's smile is proportional to the brightness of the spotlights.

To prove that everyone is important to God, the apostle Paul wrote a letter to slaves, the lowest class in his society. If anyone thought that life was meaningless, it was a slave. Slaves weren't considered people, but property. In spite of opinions to the contrary, Paul informed slaves that their jobs were important and that their lives could count for eternity. He said, "Whatever you do, do your work heartily, as for the Lord rather than for men, knowing that from the Lord you will receive the reward of the inheritance. It is the Lord Christ whom you serve" (Colossians 3:23–24).

Your life can also count for eternity. Don't you think that there's more to this life than bringing home a paycheck and finding things to do in your spare time? A hundred years from now the things that currently charm you will mean nothing. Could there be a divine purpose for your life beyond this earthly existence? I believe there is.

If you want to make sense of this life on earth, you must understand that God has a plan. Life is worth living because God has a blueprint for eternity. It began in eternity past, unfolds on planet earth, and will continue in eternity future.

GOD'S ETERNAL PLAN

In eternity past, God decided that He wanted to have a family, a group of people that He could call His own. He would never force anyone to become a part of His family. Instead, He would choose those who wanted to love Him forever.

God created a temporary world called earth, then placed people on the planet to populate it and live for a short time on it. During their earthly lives, people decide if they want to spend eternity with Him. Those who reject His companionship don't have the privilege of spending eternity with Him in heaven, but for those who love Him, God has made a never-ending kingdom. Planet earth is a place of training to prepare His children for their eternal home.

We won't be strumming harps or eating angel food cake in heaven. God will assign us important duties in the next life. I believe the decisions you make while on earth will determine what you'll be doing in eternity. Life on earth is your Test. If you choose to be in His family, He will assign you responsibilities in heaven according to the way you live your earthly life. As you will soon discover, *you can make today count for eternity.*

But wait—you haven't entered eternity yet. If you are not in His family, you still have the opportunity to become one of His children. And there's still time to correct your life's direction and make God smile. Because when He smiles, you'll smile too.

You are on the verge of one of the greatest spiritual breakthroughs you could ever imagine. By faithfully living for God during your brief time on earth, you will change your eternal destiny.

Your eternity is still under construction!

MAKING THE MOST OF YOUR OPPORTUNITY

- Make a list of things that make God smile—things that go unnoticed by most people. Post this list on your bathroom mirror as a daily reminder of different ways you can please God throughout the week.
- To make God smile, you must first be His. Chapter 2 tells you how you can be absolutely sure that you are a child of God and part of His eternal family.

chapter two

Joining God's Family

"No one comes to the Father but through Me."

John 14:6

The phone rang at 1 A.M. in the home of Leo Winters, a highly acclaimed Chicago surgeon. The caller from the hospital said that a young boy had been tragically mangled in a late-night accident. Dr. Winters' hands were probably the only ones in the city skilled enough to save the boy.

The quickest route to the hospital took the doctor through a dangerous neighborhood. But since time was critical, he decided to take the risk. Driving through the worst part of the neighborhood, he came to a stoplight. A man in a gray hat and dirty flannel shirt jerked open the door, pulled him out of his seat, and screamed, "Give me your car!"

Winters tried to explain that he was a doctor on an emergency call, but the thief refused to listen. He jumped in the car and sped off. The doctor wandered for more than forty-five minutes, looking for a phone so he could call a taxi. When he finally got to the hospital, more than an hour had passed. Dr. Winters burst through the hospital doors and ran to the nurses' station.

The nurse on duty shook her head. "I'm sorry, doctor, but you're too late. The boy died about thirty minutes ago. His father is in the chapel if you want to see him. He is awfully upset. He couldn't understand why you never came to help."

Dr. Winters walked hurriedly down the hallway and entered the chapel. Weeping at the altar was a man dressed in a dirty flannel shirt and gray hat. Through tear-blurred eyes the boy's father looked up at the doctor and in horror realized his tragic mistake. He had foolishly pushed away the only one in the city who could have saved his son![1]

THE GHOST OF GUILT

Only one person can save your soul. When you exit this life at death, you will enter the unseen, eternal realm. For you to be admitted into heaven, God must forgive all your sins before you die. "There is a problem—your sins have cut you off from God. Because of your sin, he has turned away and will not listen anymore" (Isaiah 59:2, NLT).

Sin is the poison. Jesus is the antidote. The blood of Christ is the only cure for the sin problem. The ghost of guilt will continue to haunt you until you receive Jesus' forgiveness for your sins.

Shortly before the Reformation, Martin Luther was in his monk's cell, weeping because he felt guilty for the sins he had committed. Another monk nearby didn't know what to say to him, so he began reciting the Apostles' Creed.

"I believe in God the Father Almighty, Maker of heaven and

earth. And in Jesus Christ, His only Son, our Lord; who was conceived by the Holy Ghost, born of the virgin Mary, suffered under Pontius Pilate, was crucified, dead, and buried; He descended into hell; the third day He rose again from the dead, He ascended into heaven, and sitteth on the right hand of God the Father Almighty; from thence He shall come to judge the quick and the dead. I believe in the Holy Ghost, the holy Catholic church; the communion of the saints; the forgiveness of sins, the—"

"Wait!" Luther interrupted. "What did you just say?"

"What do you mean, what did I say?"

"That last part. What was that again?"

"Oh that," the monk responded. "I said, 'I believe in the forgiveness of sins.'"

"The forgiveness of sins," Luther said, as if savoring each word. *"I believe in the forgiveness of sins.* Then there is hope for me. Maybe there is a way to God."[2]

Jesus is our hope and the only way to enter the kingdom of God. He said, "I am the way, and the truth, and the life; no one comes to the Father but through Me" (John 14:6). Only Christ can cancel our spiritual debts. Jesus paid the penalty for our sins by dying on the cross.

Let's back up for a moment and examine how God prepared the world in advance for Christ's sacrificial death.

OLD TESTAMENT CREDIT CARDS

Recently my wife and I ate a meal in a restaurant and paid for it with a charge card. We enjoyed the benefits of eating dinner on credit, even though the meal hadn't actually been paid for. The credit card gave us the privilege of purchasing a product immediately by promising to pay for it in the future.

God's method of forgiveness is similar to a spiritual charge account. When we place our faith in Christ, all our debts of sin are transferred to His bill.

People living during Old Testament times charged their sins on spiritual credit cards through animal sacrifices. They took their VISA (Very Important Sacrifice of Animals) cards to the temple in Jerusalem where the transaction took place. The priests, or store clerks, sacrificed the animals on the altar, and the clients' sins were credited by faith on the future Messiah's bill. They were able to experience the blessing of forgiveness even though Christ hadn't yet died for their sins. They "charged" their sins to the account of the Savior, who would one day come to pay off the bill.

God established the sacrificial system to teach people that He takes sin seriously. By offering the animals on the altar, the worshipers learned that something must die to pay for their sins. Even though millions of animals were sacrificed over the centuries, not one drop of their blood was able to cleanse anyone from sin: "It is impossible for the blood of bulls and goats to take away sins" (Hebrews 10:4).

Old Testament credit cards had no intrinsic value, just as the plastic cards in our wallets are worthless in and of themselves. God instituted the offerings as an object lesson to teach His people about the Lamb of God who would take away the sins of the world (John 1:29). Without the system of animal sacrifice, they would never have understood why Jesus had to die for their sins.

Over the centuries, the credit card bill continued to grow. Trillions of sins and transgressions were committed and millions of animals were sacrificed. The national debt was becoming enormous. Someone needed to pay the bill, but who?

Buddhism teaches that you can pay off your own bill by being good. However, only a perfect person can eradicate this debt. The sins of the world weren't charged to The Buddha's account, and he never volunteered to pay the bill. Hinduism sings the same song, different verse. Hinduism's "Path of Works" attempts to eradicate the debt through rites, ceremonies, and duties. And then Mohammed came along, but he didn't offer to pick up the tab, either.

Of all the religious leaders in history, only Jesus Christ gave Himself as a payment for sins. He came to earth for the express purpose of paying the debt of sins against God.

Jesus lived a sinless life, which qualified Him to be the spotless Lamb who would be sacrificed for all mankind. "You know that He appeared in order *to take away sins;* and in Him there is no sin" (1 John 3:5). As He was dying on the cross He cried out, "It is finished," which can also be translated "paid in full."

Jesus reached out with one hand to gather all past sins; with the other, He gathered all our future sins. Then, once for all, He died to cancel the debt. "But He, having offered *one sacrifice for sins for all time,* SAT DOWN AT THE RIGHT HAND OF GOD" (Hebrews 10:12).

Then He took His blood into the holy place in heaven to obtain our eternal redemption:

> He entered through *the greater and more perfect tabernacle,* not made with hands, that is to say, not of this creation...*through His own blood, He entered the holy place* once for all, having obtained eternal redemption. (Hebrews 9:11–12)

Moses' tabernacle was merely an earthly model that God gave so we could understand how Christ's blood was presented in the holy place in heaven. Now that Jesus has obtained eternal redemption through His blood, animal sacrifices aren't needed anymore.

RECEIVING GOD'S GIFT

Most people, if they are honest, will admit that they feel terribly guilty and in need of God's forgiveness for things they have done. Do you feel that way, too? Although you don't deserve the gift of salvation—no one does—God wants you to receive it. Will you let Him take away your sins once and for all?

Salvation is not based on our good works, but on God's great mercy. "God saved you by his special favor when you believed. And you can't take credit for this; *it is a gift from God.* Salvation is not a reward for the good things we have done, so none of us can boast about it" (Ephesians 2:8–9, NLT).

Salvation is not based

on our good works,

but on God's great mercy.

Jesus has already paid for your sins. He canceled your debt at the cross. But like a ticket that's been purchased for you, it's not truly *yours* until you accept it. So now the only thing left is for you to receive Jesus' free gift of forgiveness. Each person must individually receive Jesus Christ as Lord and Savior. He won't force His forgiveness on anyone. Don't take this decision lightly. Your acceptance or rejection of Christ's sacrificial death will decide your eternal destiny.

Because God is holy, He must judge sin. When people reject God's payment for their sins, they must pay the penalty themselves in hell. The good news is that God loves us so much that He made a way to escape hell. "God demonstrates His own love toward us, in that while we were yet sinners, Christ died for us" (Romans 5:8). How did this loving God demonstrate His love for us? Not by ignoring our sins or by abolishing hell, but by providing the way of salvation through Christ's death. God doesn't want anyone to perish, but for all to come to repentance (2 Peter 3:9). He longs for you to be one of His chosen people so you can spend eternity with Him in heaven.

You can receive salvation only while you are alive. Many people plan a deathbed conversion. The problem is that we never know when we will die. "Behold, now is 'THE ACCEPTABLE TIME,' behold, now is 'THE DAY OF SALVATION'" (2 Corinthians 6:2). There's no need to wait any longer. You can receive eternal life right now by praying this:

> *Heavenly Father, I realize that I am*
> *a sinner and need Your forgiveness.*
> *I want to spend eternity with You.*
> *Jesus, thank You for dying on the cross for my sins.*
> *I invite You to come into my heart and save me.*
> *Wash me clean from every sin with Your blood.*
> *I give my life to You. Amen.*

YOUR NEW ETERNAL DESTINY

If you prayed that prayer, your eternal destiny has just changed! You are now a child of God, one of His chosen people, and you have entered God's kingdom. Your spiritual debts have been forgiven, and heaven is your new eternal home. Welcome to the family of God! Go tell someone what you've done and find a church where you can learn more about your Savior.

Now God has a new script for you to follow for your remaining years on earth. He has exciting things charted for you, and He will help you follow that plan. The Holy Spirit, who has just now come to live inside you, will guide you through this life and give you the power to live for God.

As you serve the Lord, keep in mind that your good deeds won't make you any more acceptable to Him. God has already accepted you through Jesus Christ. However, you can make every remaining day on earth count for eternity by joyfully serving Him. God promises to personally reward those who live to please Him. While salvation determines your eternal *destination,* how you live after being saved will decide your eternal *occupation.*

God is not finished with you yet. Your eternity is still in the making. As you will soon discover, by making God smile you will receive even greater blessings in your permanent home, heaven. The rest of your life can be the best of your life.

MAKING THE MOST OF YOUR OPPORTUNITY

- Write down in this book or in the back of your Bible the date and place that you prayed to receive Jesus Christ. If you ever doubt your salvation experience, go back and look at what you have written.

- Begin each day by praying, *Lord, thank You for saving me and giving me another day of life on planet earth. Show me how to live this day for You.*

THE UNSEEN WORLD

Jesus answered, "My kingdom is not of this world."

JOHN 18:36

I n the movie *The Truman Show*, Truman Burbank thinks that his life is no different from anyone else's—until he begins to notice peculiar things happening, like events repeating themselves every day. Then he gets suspicious that something strange is going on.

What he doesn't realize is that every second of his life from the day he was born has been telecast live to the entire planet. He is the star of *The Truman Show*, the most popular television show in the world, which broadcasts every aspect of his life around the clock. From the moment he wakes up until he goes to bed at night, the world eavesdrops on Truman's life through the aid of five thousand hidden cameras. Finally Truman comes to the life-changing realization that an unseen audience is watching his every move.

Do you realize that an unseen audience is watching your life, too? Not through television cameras, but through the eyes of God. Although we can't see Him, God is watching everything we do. "And there is no creature hidden from His sight, but all things are open and laid bare to the eyes of Him with whom we have to do" (Hebrews 4:13).

Why is God keeping an eye on us? He wants to help us live triumphantly. "For the eyes of the LORD move to and fro throughout the earth that He may strongly support those whose heart is completely His" (2 Chronicles 16:9). He is seeking to support those who bring a smile to His face. We can have a personal relationship with the God of heaven, even though we can't see Him (1 Peter 1:8).

An unseen world exists beyond this earthly realm. When God created the universe, He made two kinds of things: objects that are visible and objects that are invisible.

For by Him all things were created, both *in the heavens and on earth, visible and invisible,* whether thrones or dominions or rulers or authorities—all things have been created through Him and for Him. (Colossians 1:16)

The things we see are temporal, but invisible things are eternal (2 Corinthians 4:18). Everything in this world will eventually be destroyed, but the unseen world will last forever.

If you believe only in the things you see, you will never be able to comprehend the next life. Jesus explained to Pontius Pilate that His kingdom exists in another world (John 18:36). If Pilate had heeded Christ's words about the unseen kingdom, he would not have crucified the Lord (1 Corinthians 2:8).

What kind of words can we use to describe a kingdom we've never seen? Trying to envision life after death is like a baby in the womb trying to figure out what life will be like after birth. He has never seen a tree, dog, car, or even another person. Because these concepts haven't yet entered his mind, he won't understand them until after he has been born. Likewise, we won't completely understand the details about the kingdom of heaven until we get there.

However, it is possible to believe in things that we cannot see. After His resurrection, Jesus said, "Blessed are they that have not seen, and yet have believed" (John 20:29, KJV). In fact, that is the definition of faith. It is "the evidence of things not seen" (Hebrews 11:1, KJV). Through faith we can believe in things that we can't see, based upon God's revelation that they do indeed exist.

Through faith we can believe in things that we can't see, based upon God's revelation that they do indeed exist.

We can believe in things we can't see by gathering convincing information from sources other than sight. Jesus Christ is our trustworthy source for believing in unseen things. One reason He came from heaven was to tell us what lies ahead in eternity. Then He paved the way to heaven for us by dying for our sins and rising from the dead. After His resurrection, He ascended into heaven to prepare an eternal home for us (John 14:2). Jesus didn't go to all this trouble to hide heaven from us, but to reveal it.

However, God won't reveal His entire blueprint for eternity because we could never understand it at our current level of intelligence. At present we "see through a glass, darkly" (1 Corinthians 13:12, KJV). But when we stand face-to-face with God Himself, our intelligence will be expanded so that we can see the complete picture of the next world.

Unfortunately, our knowledge will be limited until that day. We can't yet fathom what we will be doing in heaven for eternity. Our minds would have to go through a time warp even to begin to grasp concepts about God's eternal kingdom.

Is there any way that we can find clues to what will take place in the unseen world? I think there is.

BACK TO THE PAST

In January 1896, a time capsule was buried in a certain community. Instructions were left saying that the box should be opened exactly one hundred years later. In January 1996, the container was unearthed. Inside were a number of discolored letters written to people living in a future century. Although the writers knew that they would die long before the capsule was opened, they neverthe-less addressed questions to readers who hadn't yet been born. One letter asked, "Has anyone invented a flying machine yet?"

Suppose you could send a letter *back* in time to those people. They would be astonished to read your reply: "People travel all over the world in flying machines every day. Men have flown to the moon and back. The U.S. space probe *Pioneer 10* has flown past the planet Pluto, which is 5.9 billion miles from the sun. The *Hubble* space telescope gives us images of stars and galaxies at the farthest reaches of the universe, and in our living rooms we see the pictures on television. On TV we can watch events taking place all over the world." You conclude the letter by mentioning computers, the Internet, lasers, DNA, and cellular phones.

What would those nineteenth-century folks think of your let-ter? How would they make heads or tails of it? For your letter to make sense, you would have to use words they could understand. References to satellites and computers wouldn't mean anything to them. Although you could provide them with many more details about advancements in technology, you would have to limit the information you revealed. In other words, because you are limited to the simplest of terms, all you could give them would be a vague idea of what their future was going to look like.

In the same way, when God writes to us about what happens in the future, He must speak in elementary terms. He informs us that in eternity future, we will supervise "many things," manage "true riches," and "serve Him" forever. Although that doesn't tell us much, rest assured that these phrases speak of magnificent adventures in the next life. God could give us many exciting details about eternity, but we wouldn't understand them. Instead of confusing us, He has chosen to reveal some truths about eternity on a kindergarten level.

BACK TO THE BASICS

It's your first day in kindergarten. You put your Donald Duck lunch box in your assigned cubbyhole and sit at your desk. You are anxious to get out your crayons and begin solving the world's problems. It's the first day of school, and you're going to try your hardest to color inside the lines.

But instead of passing out papers to color, the teacher hands out textbooks on physics, chemistry, and computer programming. "I expect you to have every book read by Friday," she announces to the class. "We will have a test to find out how well you understand these subjects."

You are horrified! You haven't even learned to read yet. You don't know how to count past twenty, and you're not even sure that you can recite your ABCs correctly. The little girl at the desk next to you cries out, "I want my mommy!"

The time will come when you will be able to comprehend physics, chemistry, and computer programming, but you aren't capable of understanding them at a kindergarten level of learning. Instead, the instructor needs to teach you the alphabet and how to count—the basic things you need to know in order to understand more complex thoughts later. In the future, after you've grasped the elementary principles, you can progress to more advanced ideas. Would you ever have guessed when you were in kindergarten that you would someday understand the things you now know?

Planet earth is the kindergarten class where we learn basic ideas about the future He has in store for us.

BACK TO THE FUTURE

I believe that God wants to reveal some truths to us about our destiny. Although He doesn't give us all the details about eternity, He has given us a general idea about what lies ahead for us.

It's no accident that things look the way they do in this world. God specifically designed certain earthly objects and relationships to help us understand the unseen world.

> For since the creation of the world His *invisible* attributes, His *eternal* power and divine nature, have been clearly seen, *being understood through what has been made,* so that they are without excuse. (Romans 1:20)

To understand heavenly truths, we must first lay hold of some earthly concepts. Jesus said, "If I told you earthly things and you do not believe, how will you believe if I tell you heavenly things?" (John 3:12). God purposely designed objects, roles, and positions in this world as models to instruct us about what will happen in the

Things Seen— On Earth	Things Not Seen— In Heaven	Reference
Temporary	Eternal	2 Corinthians 4:18
Moses' tabernacle	Tabernacle in heaven	Hebrews 8:5
Unrighteous money	True riches	Luke 16:11
Earthly jobs	Heavenly assignments	Matthew 25: 21, 23
Perishable wreaths	Imperishable wreaths	1 Corinthians 9:25
Earthly bodies	Heavenly bodies	1 Corinthians 15:40

next life. God uses things that are *seen* on earth to instruct us about some things in heaven that are *not seen*.

The chart above compares these seen and unseen things.

The Tabernacle

God told Moses to build the tabernacle as an exact replica of the one in heaven. The tabernacle served as a "copy and shadow of *the heavenly things*" (Hebrews 8:5). For centuries a goat was killed on the Day of Atonement, and the high priest sprinkled the animal's blood in the holy place.

After Jesus died for our sins, He entered heaven with His own blood and sprinkled it in the heavenly tabernacle to purchase redemption for us.

> But when Christ appeared as a high priest of the good things to come, He entered through the greater and more *perfect tabernacle, not made with hands,* that is to say, *not of*

this creation…but through His own blood, He entered the holy place once for all, having obtained eternal redemption. (Hebrews 9:11–12)

How did God show us how Christ presented His blood in the heavenly tabernacle? By using Moses' earthly tabernacle as a model. By understanding the earthly concept, we learn about heavenly things. See how the things seen have taught us about things unseen?

Money

Civilizations have used some form of money since ancient times. God uses the metaphor of money to help us understand something about managing wealth in heaven. Jesus said, "Therefore if you have not been faithful in the use of unrighteous wealth, who will entrust the *true riches* to you?" (Luke 16:11).

Managing earthly money is practice for handling "true riches" in heaven. We will examine these true riches more carefully in another chapter.

Jobs

I believe that one reason God established earthly jobs was to train us for our responsibilities in eternity. Our faithfulness and attitudes in performing our earthly jobs may well be a factor in assigning our heavenly duties. If we are faithful with a "few things" on earth, God will put us in charge of "many things" in eternity (Matthew 25:21, 23).

Rewards

Paul compares rewards on earth to rewards in heaven:

> Everyone who competes in the games exercises self-control
> in all things. They then do it to receive a perishable wreath,
> but we an imperishable. (1 Corinthians 9:25)

Paul informs us that crowns also exist in heaven and that they will be awarded to those who faithfully live for the Lord.

Bodies

We live in physical bodies now, but one day we will receive eternal bodies. "There are also heavenly bodies and earthly bodies, but the glory of the heavenly is one, and the glory of the earthly is another" (1 Corinthians 15:40). Our earthly bodies are like a caterpillar before it goes into a cocoon and is transformed into a butterfly. "Just as we have borne the image of the earthy, we will also bear the image of the heavenly" (1 Corinthians 15:49).

I could list more examples—homes, marriage, father/child relationships, military service—but I think you see the similarities. There is so much we can learn about heaven by taking a closer look at God's creation.

The earthly realm is designed to give us a general idea about heaven. Although God doesn't reveal all the details about what will happen in eternity future, He does give us enough information to understand how life on earth fits into the big picture.

Are you ready to learn more about this unseen world?

Making the Most of Your Opportunity

- List some other examples of how God uses earthly models to teach us about heavenly things.
- Design requires a designer. Check out a biology book from the library, and as you read about the complexity of life, think about its wonderful Designer.

chapter four

LIFE IS A TEST AND ONLY A TEST

"Do business with this until I come back."

LUKE 19:13

The sign in the store window read, "Boy wanted." A young man walked into the store, applied for the job, and was hired. Mr. Peters, the storeowner, instructed him to go into the attic of the building. "You will find a long, deep box up there," he said. "I want you to sort through the contents and see what should be saved."

The boy went into the attic and began sorting through the old box of junk. Not much later he came downstairs, complaining that the attic was hot and that he didn't want to finish the job. At the end of the day, Mr. Peters paid the boy and told him not to return.

The next day the sign went up in the window again. A boy named Crawford Hill came into the store to apply for the job. Mr.

Peters hired him and sent him to the attic to sort through the articles in the box.

Crawford spent hours looking through the box, separating usable nails and screws from things that should be thrown away. When he picked up one of the last items in the box, he noticed a twenty-dollar bill lying on the bottom. He grabbed the bill, raced downstairs, and said, "Look, Mr. Peters! Look what I found in the box—twenty dollars!" Then he handed the money to his boss. Mr. Peters smiled because he knew that he could trust the boy to work in his store.

The old junk box was merely a test. Mr. Peters had filled it with nails, screws, and other items to test his employee's faithfulness. He wanted to see if the boy would complete the job and keep a good attitude, even though he didn't understand why he was doing seemingly useless work. Mr. Peters had also planted a twenty-dollar bill at the bottom of the box to test his employee's honesty. If the boy didn't report finding the money, how could Mr. Peters trust him with the cash register?

By finishing the job in the hot attic and giving the money to his boss rather than pocketing it, Crawford proved that he was both faithful and honest. Years later, when Mr. Peters retired, he turned his business over to Crawford to manage.

Did you know that life on earth is also a test? All our earthly responsibilities—even the ones that seem insignificant—are in the old junk box in the attic. God is watching us to see if we will faithfully sort through life's experiences, keeping the good, throwing out the junk, exhibiting a positive attitude when we don't understand, and finishing our work. If we prove ourselves to be good and faithful during our earthly Test, God will grant us far greater duties in the next life.

Mina League

We can gain insight into God's eternal plan for His children from Jesus' parable of the minas. A mina was a bag of coins, usually silver, that weighed approximately one pound. (They are called "pounds" in the King James Version.)

> "A nobleman went to a distant country to receive a kingdom for himself, and then return. And he called ten of his slaves, and gave them ten minas and said to them, 'Do business with this until I come back.'" (Luke 19:12–13)

The nobleman told the slaves to do business while he was away. Although the slaves had identical resources, they produced different amounts. One slave gained a profit of ten more minas, while another slave made five.

When the nobleman returned after receiving his kingdom, he rewarded the slave who made ten minas by giving him authority over ten cities (Luke 19:17). He put the slave who produced five minas in charge of five cities. Their rewards were directly proportional to their productivity. The minas were simply a test to prepare them for much greater assignments, just like Mr. Peters's junk box tested Crawford Hill's faithfulness.

I think it's significant that the master rewarded these slaves *after* he received the kingdom for himself. Could it be that these cities are located in the kingdom that the master received? If the nobleman receiving the kingdom refers to Christ's second coming, then the rewards would pertain to the next life. If that's the case, as many Bible scholars believe, then one of the main reasons for our earthly existence is to get us ready for the next world.

The mina league—our earthly responsibilities—prepares us for the major league—our eternal responsibilities in God's kingdom. Whoever makes full and faithful use of opportunities for the Lord's service here will be blessed more richly in eternity.[1]

Elsa Raud writes:

The only time God has to prepare his rulers is this brief life on earth. Our training is made up of continual tests of obedience, some of them weighty, some of them apparently trivial, but how important they really are. We are being trained to do as the Lord commands, no matter what it costs us. Rulers in the eternal kingdom will be examples of prompt, wholehearted obedience.[2]

Our earthly lives serve a dual purpose. We are carrying out God's will to please Him in everything we do, but we are also in training for our eternal assignments. Earth is our temporary world to prepare us for the everlasting kingdom. "The world is passing away...but the one who does the will of God lives forever" (1 John 2:17). By living each day to please God, we can make today count for eternity. This is why we need to view our lives not in terms of seventy or eighty years on earth, but in light of forever. The end of this life is the beginning of the next.

Earth is our temporary world to prepare us for the everlasting kingdom.

GETTING THE BIG PICTURE

Suppose you sit down to read a book. It begins, "It was a dark and stormy night." You stare at the first letter, trying to figure out what *I* means. It makes no sense, so you move on to the second letter, *t.*

"I wonder what the author means by *t,*" you say. "*I...t.* Oh! He means *it!* Now we are getting somewhere." Then you closely examine the next letter, *w.* After thirty minutes of this, you still haven't made it through the first sentence. Why? Your perspective is too small.

You can expand your understanding if you will read words instead of letters. You will enlarge it even more if you will read complete sentences instead of individual words. If you want to acquire the big picture, you must read paragraphs, then chapters, and finally the whole book.

Too many of us view our life experiences from the "letter" perspective. We place our situations under a microscope and dissect each detail, completely forgetting about how everything fits into God's plan. But if we see the big picture first, the little pieces start making sense. Life becomes amazingly clear when we view it from an eternal perspective.

Keep this eternal outlook in mind as you work through life's difficulties. Never forget that your calling extends beyond this present world. When the Corinthians were struggling to make correct decisions, Paul reminded them of their eternal calling and destiny:

Or do you not know that the saints will judge the world? If the world is judged by you, are you not competent to constitute the smallest law courts? Do you not know that we will judge angels? How much more matters of *this life?* (1 Corinthians 6:2–3)

Paul informs us that in the next life we will judge angels. I'm not sure exactly what that means, but it suggests that heavenly assignments will be far more advanced than anything in this life. If that's our destiny, we should be able to carry out our earthly responsibilities, which are trivial in comparison.

We are in training for something spectacular in the next world. God has placed His children all over the world and equipped us with varying abilities to accomplish His purposes on earth. Although our everyday duties often seem mundane and routine, some have great importance in God's eyes. We are in the process of sorting through the junk box in the attic.

If we are faithful in managing our responsibilities here on earth, God will entrust us with His eternal treasures in heaven. Jesus said, "Therefore if you have not been faithful in the use of unrighteous wealth, who will entrust the *true riches* to you?" (Luke 16:11). I believe that these true riches are our rewards—our eternal assignments. Before we manage true riches, we must be faithful with the minas we are handling in this life.

George Boldt worked faithfully for years at the front desk in a small hotel. One day an elderly couple walked into the lobby and asked for a place to stay. Every room in the hotel—and every hotel in town—was occupied. Realizing that the elderly couple had nowhere to sleep, Boldt offered them his own room. Although they were reluctant to accept his offer, they eventually did so because George insisted.

The next morning when the couple was checking out, the elderly man said to George, "You're the kind of man who should be managing the best hotel in the country. Someday I'm going to build that hotel and let you manage it."

Several years later, Boldt received a letter in the mail. It contained a round-trip ticket and a note from the man to whom he had given his room years before. The man invited George to visit him in New York City.

When Boldt arrived in New York, the gentleman took him to a downtown corner where a huge building stood. "George, this is the hotel I built for you to manage."

Boldt stared in amazement at the glorious structure. The hotel was the Waldorf-Astoria! The elderly man was William Waldorf Astor, one of the wealthiest men in the country. Boldt's faithfulness in managing a small hotel had prepared him to manage one of the most magnificent hotels this country has ever seen.

The few brief moments you live on earth will determine your responsibilities for all eternity.

On judgment day, God will examine how well we managed our lives on earth. If we were faithful in fulfilling our responsibilities in this life, He will assign us greater things to manage in the next life.

God wants you to realize the significance of your earthly existence so you can live up to your fullest potential. Don't believe the lie that your life isn't important. The few brief moments you live on earth will determine your responsibilities for all eternity. You only get one shot at living on planet earth—your Opportunity.

If you maintain your integrity and keep sorting through life's junk box, you'll pass the test. And there just might be a promotion waiting for you in the next world!

MAKING THE MOST OF YOUR OPPORTUNITY

- What are some of the responsibilities in your junk box? Are you exhibiting a positive attitude toward God and others, even when some things in your life don't make sense?
- In what ways can you get a bigger picture of your earthly responsibilities?

chapter five

The Opportunity beyond a Lifetime

"Well done, good and faithful slave."

MATTHEW 25:23

K ent and Barbara Hughes attended a school Christmas play in which their daughter, Holly, played the lead character in O. Henry's *The Gift of the Magi*. Holly charmed the audience with her acting ability. Kent and Barbara enthusiastically applauded her brilliant performance.

Immediately after Holly's play concluded, Kent and Barbara watched their son's Christmas play. Unlike his sister, Kent Jr. wasn't assigned the lead part. Because he had a learning disability, he was given a minor role with only four lines.

Kent Jr. had had an extremely difficult time memorizing his part. He had worked on learning his four lines from Thanksgiving until Christmas. When the family went on trips, they worked with him to help him memorize his sentences. Everyone in the car learned the lines backwards and forwards, but Kent never said them correctly. Not one time.

Now it was time for the play to begin. The curtains pulled back. Kent Sr. and Barbara sat nervously on the edge of their seats. The spotlight shone down on their son, who still didn't know his lines. After hesitating for an excruciating moment, Kent Jr. lifted his voice and said, "Strange feelings come upon me, though I know not why. The night is still around me; the stars shine in the sky."

For the first time, he quoted his lines perfectly! Though no one in the audience applauded, Kent Sr. and Barbara silently gave him a standing ovation. They were elated with their son's performance.[1]

Holly played the lead role; Kent Jr. had only a minor part. Although they had different levels of ability, the two children were equally pleasing to their parents.

LEAD PARTS AND MINOR ROLES

If life on earth is a test, then why isn't everyone playing on a level field? When some people have greater abilities and opportunities than others, they appear to have an unfair advantage. Why do some people have incredible gifts, while others have disabilities?

George Orwell once wrote, "All [people] are equal, but some more equal than others." While we all have equal worth, we don't have equal abilities. Some people have lead parts in life. Others have minor roles.

God calls His children to a wide variety of assignments. Some are commissioned to be missionaries, while others are called to be mechanics. Our world would be in trouble if no one knew how to repair vehicles! No matter what our abilities or professions, we can all be equally pleasing to our heavenly Father. When we use our abilities to fulfill our callings, our Father in heaven applauds enthusiastically, even if no one else notices.

Jesus told a parable that I believe explains why people have different degrees of ability. A master, about to leave on a journey, summoned his slaves and distributed money to them. In this story, the master distributed talents instead of minas. A talent was a bag of gold or silver coins weighing between eighty and ninety-five pounds. He did not distribute them equally, but unequally, according to their abilities (Matthew 25:14–21). He gave one slave five talents, another slave two, and a third slave only one.

The master entrusted the most money to the slave with the greatest aptitude and the smallest amount to the one with the least ability. By allotting his money according to their abilities, he assigned their responsibilities equitably. While the master was away on his journey, each slave had to manage the money he had been given. When the master returned, each would have to account for how he had handled it.

Some people confuse the parable of the talents with the parable of the minas, but there are a few key differences. In the parable of the minas, a nobleman entrusts the same amount of money to each of his ten slaves. In the parable of the talents, a rich man gives a different amount of money to each of his three slaves, according to their abilities.

Why did Jesus change the details in these two parables? Perhaps to emphasize different truths in each. The parable of the minas highlights the slaves' *faithfulness;* the parable of the talents accentuates the slaves' *abilities.* Although the five-talent slave and the two-talent slave had unequal abilities, they were equally pleasing to their master.

How does this truth apply to us today? No matter what our level of ability, we all have the same potential to make God smile.

The talents represent the abilities and resources God has

granted us to fulfill our callings in life. Charles Spurgeon wrote, "The talents are anything and everything that our Lord has given to us for use here as his stewards."[2]

Permit me to ask you a few questions about your "talents." Are you using your spiritual gifts to fulfill your calling? Do you make the most of your opportunities? Is your attitude positive? Do you perform your best work at your job? How do you handle your money? Do you treat others with love and respect?

Just like the slaves in the parable, we must also manage our talents until the master returns. We all have different abilities and responsibilities in life, and one day we will give an account for what we did with them (Romans 14:12).

We don't all have the same *ability*—talents and skills.

We don't all have the same *responsibility*—duties or obligations.

But we all have the same *accountability*—we must all answer to God for how we used our abilities to fulfill our responsibilities. That puts everyone on a level playing field.

THE ENVY TRAP

Do you envy those with greater abilities? If we don't understand that God distributes gifts to each person as He wills, we will complain about how little we have and envy those who have more.

The one-talent person envies the two-talent man and says, "I don't have much, so I don't have to be responsible for it."

The two-talent man who longs to be a five-talent person says, "Why did the five-talent slave receive more than twice what I have? That's not fair."

And the five-talent man says, "Why do I have so much responsibility placed on me? I wish I were a two-talent man. He's got it easy."

We must quit comparing talents and start being faithful with what has been entrusted to us.

When the rich man returned from his journey, he asked the slaves to explain what they had done with his money. The master didn't expect the two-talent man to produce five talents. God is not unreasonable. He doesn't expect results that are greater than the potential He has given us. But neither does He expect results that are less than the potential He has given us. He expects us to use our abilities to the maximum. He expects five-talent people to produce more than two-talent people.

The more a person is given, the more that will be required of that person (Luke 12:48). Unfortunately, many five-talent people put forth a two-talent effort. Are you using your God-given abilities to the maximum?

Although we all have different abilities and responsibilities, we can all be equally pleasing to God. The two-talent and five-talent slaves were equally faithful, and the master gave them identical praise:

"Well done, good and faithful slave. You were faithful with a few things, I will put you in charge of many things; enter into the joy of your master." (Matthew 25:21, 23)

The two-talent slave and the five-talent slave received the same reward because they both reached their highest potential.

God won't evaluate us according to how many talents we have, but by how we use them to fulfill our responsibilities. A person who faithfully teaches a Sunday school class for children may receive the same—or greater—eternal reward as a pastor who faithfully preaches to a large congregation. Rather than envying those with greater abilities and opportunities, we need to concentrate on making better use of our own God-given talents.

One-Talent People

One other slave is mentioned in this parable: "But he who received the one talent went away, and dug a hole in the ground and hid his master's money" (Matthew 25:18). The one-talent man is a glaring reminder that a negative attitude can cause us to bury our talents. His master called him a "wicked, lazy slave" (v. 26). This doesn't mean that the person with the least ability is the most wicked. The one-talent slave had the lightest load among the slaves, yet he shirked his responsibility and hid his talent in the ground.

When his master returned, the one-talent slave had to give account, just like the two-talent and five-talent slaves did. He dug up the money, returned it to his master, and gave an excuse for not investing it:

> "Master, I knew you to be a hard man, reaping where you did not sow and gathering where you scattered no seed. And I was afraid, and went away and hid your talent in the ground. See, you have what is yours." (Matthew 25:24–25)

The master was furious that the one-talent slave had not used his single talent to produce another one. It wasn't much to ask. The least he could have done was to have put the money in the bank to draw some interest (v. 27). As long as his talent was buried, it couldn't produce anything. The effect was the same as if the master hadn't given him any money to begin with. If we aren't using our abilities to glorify God, it's the same as not having them.

One-talent people are notorious for burying their talents. They believe that they can't make a major contribution with their minor abilities, so they don't do anything. Millions of talents are buried all over the world right now simply because one-talent people refuse to put their abilities to work. Do you feel sorry for yourself because you assume that your one talent isn't enough?

Trey Wood was born with only one arm. Most people assumed that his handicap would prevent him from participating in a sport like football. Instead of feeling sorry for himself, Trey decided to prove the experts wrong. Not only did he learn to play football, but he also received an athletic scholarship to Sam Houston State University. He went beyond expectations and earned a starting position as a defensive back. One of his responsibilities was to knock down passes when the football was thrown in his area.

Another one-armed young man named Dawuan Miller also had a dream to play football. In spite of his disability he, too, earned a scholarship and became the starting defensive back for Boise State University.

Both players made first team. Both excelled at their positions. Despite lacking an arm, Wood broke the career record for Sam Houston State with eleven blocked kicks. Dawuan silenced the doubters by using his one arm to intercept two passes in playoff games.

On September 16, 1995, Sam Houston State played Boise State in football. For the first time in the history of the sport, two colleges played a game with one-armed defensive backs starting for each team. Few will remember the score of the game, but no one who was there will forget how two one-armed players' gutsy performances overshadowed the rest of the talent on the field.

Each of these two football players did more with one arm than most people do with two. When one-talent people apply themselves, they can accomplish incredible feats. You can do amazing things with just one talent, if you will dare to believe it.

Do you have two arms, or just one? Two talents, or just one? Don't feel sorry for yourself. You can prove the experts wrong if you will develop your abilities to the maximum.

WHY PEOPLE BURY THEIR TALENTS

Why did the one-talent slave bury his money? He had a wicked heart, which distorted his view of his master. "I knew you to be a hard man," he said. His twisted perspective of his master caused him to react with animosity. His outlook was warped in a couple of ways.

First, he had a wrong concept of the *character* of his master. Despite what the slave believed, the rich man wasn't a hard master, but a very kind one. He generously rewarded the two other slaves because their faithfulness pleased him. The one-talent slave didn't understand his master's heart. If he had known his master better—that he was kind and generous—he would not have been afraid of him and buried his talent.

Everything we do *for* God is based upon our concept *of* God. If we believe He is hard, we will hide our talents. If we believe He is merciful, we will multiply our talents.

> *Everything we do* for *God is based upon our concept* of *God.*

Second, the one-talent slave had a wrong concept of the *motive* of his master. He saw him as greedy, "reaping where you did not sow and gathering where you scattered no seed." The wicked slave believed that the master made his slaves work only so he could profit. But the master wanted them to work hard so *they* could profit. His purpose for entrusting talents to them was so he could reward them after he returned from his long journey.

But the one-talent slave didn't have a clue about the master's plan to reward his labor. His negative opinion of his master led him to make a terrible decision about what to do with his talent. He could have put it in a bank to draw interest, but he buried it instead. He detested his master so much that he didn't even want him to receive the interest.

Many people today also have a distorted view of God. They believe that He is a hard master who demands work just to make people miserable. The truth is that God wants us to be faithful in our work so that He can reward us throughout eternity.

The master put the five- and two-talent slaves in charge of "many things" (v. 21). If the one-talent slave had loved his master and produced one talent, he would have been promoted just like the other two slaves. Equal reward was available despite unequal gifting. Sadly, the one-talent slave who despised his master was delivered to the place of "weeping and gnashing of teeth" (Matthew 25:30).

ABILITIES	THIS LIFE	THE NEXT LIFE
5-talent slave	Faithful with a few things	In charge of many things in heaven
2-talent slave	Faithful with a few things	In charge of many things in heaven
1-talent slave	Wicked and lazy	Weeping and gnashing of teeth in hell

No-Talent People?

What about those who never have an opportunity to experience a full life on earth? What about babies who have died, or those who are physically disabled or mentally handicapped? How will God evaluate them?

God's way of assessing their lives is His secret. He is loving and gracious and never makes a wrong judgment. Rest assured that however God judges them, it will be just and good.

The real question is not about them, but about us. What are we doing with *our* lives? How are we using *our* talents? God doesn't offer us just the opportunity of a lifetime. He offers us an opportunity *beyond* a lifetime. Our diligence in fulfilling our callings will determine our heavenly responsibilities.

If we aren't faithful during our testing period on earth, why would God want to put us in charge of many things in heaven? If we aren't good stewards with our finances, why would God want to entrust His eternal riches to us?

We have only one window of time to change eternity. God wants to place us in charge of many things in the next life, but we have to be faithful with our talents in this life. The next section takes a brief look at what we are preparing for in eternity future. After you preview the next life, you'll understand why you shouldn't waste your Opportunity.

Making the Most of Your Opportunity

- Stop comparing yourself with others, and start making use of your own abilities and resources.
- Write down some ways that you can make better use of your talents. Remember that your Father in heaven applauds when you live to make Him smile.

part two

A Glimpse into Eternity Future

Upon your arrival in heaven, a long-faced angel meets you at the pearly gates. "We've been expecting you," he announces in a voice as gloomy as Eeyore's. "You have an appointment with God. Come with me."

As you follow the angel down the streets of gold, you pass by a large crowd. You expect to see people singing songs of celebration. Instead, you see people yawning. You are shocked to discover that not a single person is smiling. Everyone looks bored to tears. A hunchbacked man shuffles by moaning, "Oh boy, another billion years of praising the Lord. Just what I always wanted."

You then notice the twenty-four elders—the very ones you had read about in the book of Revelation. Like children being told to stay seated, they are squirming in their thrones, having been confined there for several thousand years.

Just as you're about to be ushered in, your alarm clock buzzes. To your relief, it was only a bad dream.

If heaven is like that, take me off the rolls up yonder. Thank God that heaven isn't miserable or boring—it's a place of celebration and endless ecstasy! David tells us that in God's presence we will experience ultimate fullness of joy (Psalm 16:11).

Before you read any further, please dispose of any nightmarish thoughts about heaven. Thank you.

Now let's find out the truth about this wonderful place.

chapter six

HEAVEN'S HEADLINES

God will give to each person according to what he has done.

ROMANS 2:6

I f heaven had a daily newspaper, the headlines would read quite differently than our earthly tabloids. The good deeds that don't get credit on earth would make the front page in heaven's newspaper. Take a peek at this edition of *Heaven's Headlines.*

HEAVEN'S HEADLINES
Keeping You Informed about Significant Events on Earth

Kathy S.* Changes 10,000th Diaper

Rod K.* Mows Neighbor's Grass

Tony P.* Gets Saved; Starts Tithing

Max M.* Delivers Brownies to Enemy

Dan B.* Changes Tire for Stranded Motorist

Gayle H.* Takes Meal to Sick Person

Unnamed Widow Puts Last Two Coins in Treasury Box

Last names are omitted until rewards are handed out in heaven.

Changing diapers will be rewarded in heaven? Definitely.

Taking brownies to your enemy? Yep.

Putting in your two cents worth? Yes, if you are a poor widow giving an offering. If your two cents is a prejudiced opinion, no.

We've got to start thinking differently about what matters to God. Did you know that the little things you do please Him? This means that anyone, including you, can make the headlines in heaven. It all depends on which world you love most. God not only wants to save us from hell, but also to reward us in heaven.

The subject of rewards raises questions. What is the purpose of rewards? Is it selfish to want them? Hebrews 11:6 says that God is a rewarder of those who seek *Him*, not the rewards. Our calling is to love and please God, and He will take care of the rewarding part.

Imagine a WWII soldier, wounded while courageously rescuing his fellow soldiers. When he returned home, he was rewarded with the Medal of Honor for his service. What had motivated him to put his life in danger? He risked his life to save his friends' lives and defend his country's freedom. When his life was at stake in battle, he wasn't thinking, *I'm going to put my life in jeopardy so that I will receive a medal.* The reward was simply the nation's way of showing appreciation for his heroic actions.

In the same way, we serve God because we love Him and our fellow man. We don't serve for the reward, but for the Lord. "We also have as our ambition…to be pleasing to Him" (2 Corinthians 5:9).

Rewards are simply God's way of showing that He is pleased with our lives.

"It's selfish to talk about eternal rewards," some may argue. "That'll only make you so heavenly minded that you are of no earthly good."

On the contrary, we should be heavenly minded in order to be of *more* earthly good. Jesus was the most heavenly-minded person to ever walk this planet, and He did more earthly good than anyone in history. Ironically, the "enemies of the cross...set their minds on earthly things" (Philippians 3:18–19).

Jesus would not have told us about heavenly rewards if He hadn't wanted us to know about them. He could have kept the truth about eternal rewards a big secret to be revealed to all on Judgment Day. Instead, He specifically told us that some things we do now will be rewarded in the next life.

Jesus was the most heavenly-minded person to ever walk this planet, and He did more earthly good than anyone in history.

Why did God give us so much information about rewards? I believe it's because He wants us to know that:

- another world exists beyond this life;
- our lives on earth can count toward the next life;
- when we serve Him, our labor is not in vain (1 Corinthians 15:58);
- we have a heavenly incentive when we are going through difficult times.

Since God is the creator of eternal rewards, it's not selfish to think about them. God wants us to know what awaits us in the next world. But more than that, He wants us to live now to glorify Him.

WHAT DEEDS WILL GOD REWARD?

Your name may not be recorded in the *Guinness Book of World Records* for serving God, but you can have a place in God's book of heavenly rewards. How do we know what pleases Him? Here are some Scriptures that tell us what God will reward.

Being Persecuted for Righteousness' Sake

Jesus said, "Blessed are you when people insult you and persecute you, and falsely say all kinds of evil against you because of Me. Rejoice and be glad, for *your reward in heaven is great*" (Matthew 5:11–12). Jesus said that if we experience persecution on earth, we will be rewarded in heaven.

The promise of heavenly reward has helped many people endure life's difficulties. Moses endured ill-treatment because he was looking for the heavenly reward (Hebrews 11:24–26). Paul overcame incredible adversity because he kept his eyes on the prize (Philippians 3:14). Jesus was able to endure the cross because he focused on "the joy set before Him" (Hebrews 12:2).

In a world filled with hate, distress, and despair, we need the encouragement that comes from beyond this life. "If we have hoped in Christ in this life only, we are of all men most to be pitied" (1 Corinthians 15:19). Our hope reaches into eternity, where Christ reigns over all forever.

Persecution can be anything from being slandered to being tortured. When we are being persecuted, it's tempting to think that God doesn't love us anymore. How could He allow such a thing?

Doesn't He care? Of course He does. When we're persecuted, the Lord hasn't stopped loving us—the world has started hating us.

Jesus said that when we're persecuted, we should be "glad *in that day* and leap for joy, for behold, your reward is great in heaven" (Luke 6:23). He revealed this truth about heavenly rewards to motivate us to keep the proper attitude when we are attacked for our faith. These rewards will be more wonderful than we could ever imagine. Instead of whining and complaining, we should jump for joy when we are mistreated.

When people hate us for His name's sake, we have a choice. We can focus our attention either on our earthly enemies or on our heavenly Father. If we look at our adversaries, we will want to retaliate. But if we are heavenly minded, we will have a higher tolerance for persecution.

Paul was beaten, stoned, scourged, and imprisoned, but he always kept his eyes fixed on the next world. In spite of these terrible things, he said, "For I consider that the sufferings of this present time are not worthy to be compared with the glory that is to be revealed to us" (Romans 8:18). Paul considered his earthly problems to be insignificant in light of what awaited him in heaven. "For momentary, light affliction is producing for us an eternal weight of glory far beyond all comparison" (2 Corinthians 4:17).

Once we understand what is transpiring in heaven, we realize that *our enemies are actually helping us gain eternal rewards.* Of course, our persecutors don't know this secret about God's way of blessing us eternally. If they did, they might stop harassing us.

Cheerfully Giving Money to the Lord

Jesus told us to lay up treasure in heaven, not on earth. "But store up for yourselves treasures in heaven, where neither moth nor rust destroys, and where thieves do not break in or steal; for where your treasure is, there your heart will be also" (Matthew 6:20–21). In heaven moths can't eat it, rust can't destroy it, thieves can't steal it, and the IRS can't tax it.

If we cheerfully give our offerings to the Lord, He will repay us in eternity. It takes faith to let go of something we can see in order to gain something that we can't see. But as martyred missionary Jim Elliot said, "He is no fool who gives what he cannot keep to gain what he cannot lose."

What we do with our money reveals what we love the most. If our money could talk, where would it say it had been?

A one-dollar bill met a fifty-dollar bill and said, "Hey, I haven't seen you around here much. Where have you been?"

The fifty-dollar bill answered, "Oh, I spent some time hanging around casinos and playing the lottery, and then I went on a cruise and made the rounds of the ship. I came back to the United States for a while and went to a couple of pro football games, to the mall—that kind of stuff. Where have you been?

The one-dollar bill said, "You know, same old place—church, church, church."

One day our money *will* talk because we will give an account to God for what we did with it. Although we can't see inside a person's heart, we can see where his treasure goes. When we look at our treasure, we will find our hearts right in the middle of it.

Jesus told us to invest in the futures market, so to speak, so that our hearts would be interested in the eternal rather than the temporal. He once told a wealthy man, "Go and sell all you possess and give to the poor, and you will have treasure in heaven; and come, follow Me" (Mark 10:21). He wanted the wealthy man to trade up—to exchange his earthly treasure for heavenly treasure. Because the man was earthly minded instead of heavenly minded, he went away grieved.

Money can have that effect. If our treasure is in heaven, our hearts will be there. If our investments are on earth, our hearts will be here. Our hearts and treasure are interlocked.

I know a man who invested a considerable amount of money in the stock market. When his stock went up in value, his spirit was high. But when his stock went down, he became depressed. His treasure and heart rode together in the same roller coaster car. He invested his treasure in the stock market and, sure enough, his heart was also invested in it.

Giving isn't hard if we love the object of our gift. But if we don't love the recipient of the gift, giving is extremely difficult. Although we can give without loving, we cannot love without giving. Giving our money to the Lord proves that we love Him more than the things we could have bought with it. Our offering needs to be an act of worship from our hearts. If our offering means nothing to us, it means nothing to God.

The dollar amount we give on earth is not directly proportional to the amount we'll receive in heaven. Jesus once watched many rich people put large amounts of money in the treasury. After they gave, a poor widow put two small copper coins in the treasury box. Jesus then told His disciples, "Truly I say to you, this poor widow put in more than all the contributors to the treasury" (Mark 12:43).

How can less be more? The widow only gave two small coins, but she gave a fortune according to heaven's bookkeeping system. Heaven's accountants calculate our giving based on something other than the amount we have contributed. God doesn't measure our generosity by how much we give, but by how much is left over after we give.

Do you give to the Lord's work? Are you giving with a joyful heart?

Loving Your Enemies

Do you have a hard time loving those who despise you? It's difficult because hateful actions wound us emotionally. How is it possible to love our enemies? We can start the process by praying for them.

In 1994, Cindy Hartman of Conway, Arkansas, came home and found a burglar in her house. She dropped to her knees and asked the robber if she could pray for him. "I want you to know that God loves you and that I forgive you."

The burglar came under conviction and apologized for breaking into her home. Then he yelled to his accomplice waiting in a truck outside, "We've got to unload all of this. This is a Christian family. We can't do this to them."

As Hartman remained on her knees praying for him, the thief returned the furniture he had taken from the home, took the bullets out of his gun, handed the gun to Hartman, and walked out the door.[1] Cindy literally disarmed her enemy by praying for him.

Loving our enemies isn't a natural reaction; it's a supernatural action. We can only love them through God's love inside us. Jesus said, "If you love those who love you, what credit is that to you? For even sinners love those who love them" (Luke 6:32).

We don't need to be told how to love those who love us. Anyone can do that, even the most hardened criminal. Jesus commanded us to love those who hate us. Sound hard? Just remember that He never commands us to do something that He won't enable us to do.

He also promised to reward us for it. "Love your enemies, and do good, and lend, expecting nothing in return; and *your reward will be great*" (Luke 6:35). We can only love our enemies if we view them from heaven's point of view and access God's power.

Corrie ten Boom was a prisoner in a German concentration camp during WWII. Years later, speaking in a church in Munich, she spotted in the congregation a former SS soldier who had stood guard at the shower room door at Ravensbruck. When the church was dismissed, the former Nazi came up to her and said, "How grateful I am for your message, Fräulein. To think that Jesus has washed my sins away!" He then reached out to shake her hand.

Corrie kept her hand by her side as vengeful thoughts boiled within her. Here she stood, face-to-face with the man who had been so cruel to her. She quickly prayed, *Lord Jesus, forgive me for hating him and help me to forgive him.* She tried to smile and struggled to raise her hand, but she couldn't. Again she prayed, *Jesus, I cannot forgive him. Give me Your forgiveness.*

As she slowly lifted her hand and grabbed his, an incredible thing happened:

> Into my heart sprang a love for this stranger that almost overwhelmed me. And so I discovered that it is not on our own forgiveness that the world's healing hinges. When He tells us to love our enemies, He gives, along with the command, the love itself.[2]

When we love our enemies, we are rewarded both in this life and in the life to come. On the day when the saints are rewarded, will you receive a reward for loving your enemies?

Faithfully Working at Your Job

Do you realize how important your job is in God's eyes? Did you know that God will reward you in heaven for faithfully working at it? Since you will spend approximately one-third of your life working, it makes sense that God would have a divine purpose for your professional life.

I'm convinced that your earthly job serves a double purpose: to provide for your earthly needs and to prepare you for heaven. Your eternal occupation depends in part on your faithfulness in your work on earth.

William Carey was faithful to his calling. In 1793 he went to India to start a new missionary work. He knew no one there, and he didn't know the language. When he died forty years later, he had translated the Bible into three major Indian languages, established the Baptist Union in India, founded what is now its largest newspaper, and started what is today the largest seminary in the country. Carey did more than any other individual to bring the message of Christ to that subcontinent.[3]

Although you might not be called to the mission field, you are called to be faithful at your place of employment. Be faithful to God's call, whatever it may be.

> Slaves, in all things obey those who are your masters on earth, not with external service, as those who merely please men, but with sincerity of heart, fearing the Lord. Whatever you do, do your work heartily, as for the Lord rather than for men, knowing that *from the Lord you will receive the reward* of the inheritance. *It is the Lord Christ whom you serve.* (Colossians 3:22–24)

Slaves were the lowest class of people in Roman society. In men's eyes, they were at the bottom of the barrel. They had no rights. Isn't it amazing that Jesus pointed to the slave as the premier role model for us? He said, "Whoever wishes to be first among you shall be slave of all" (Mark 10:44). Although slaves had the most insignificant of all jobs, God promised to reward them in heaven if they would work for Him instead of for men.

Do you realize the significance of this? If you think that your life doesn't count, think again. If a slave is rewarded for doing lowly .

tasks for God's glory, then so is every believer in Christ. No one is insignificant, and no job is unimportant.

Martin Luther once wrote:

> The maid who sweeps her kitchen is doing the will of God just as much as the monk who prays. The Christian shoemaker does his Christian duty—not by putting little crosses on shoes, but by making good shoes, because God is interested in good craftsmanship.[4]

The Christian mother who changes her baby's diapers will be rewarded forever for performing that duty. Don't you believe that it's God's will for a newborn to have clean diapers? Of course it is. After all, someone had to change Jesus' diapers, and I'm sure those swaddling clothes got a little messy at times. God was pleased when Mary put clean Pampers on her baby. This means that changing diapers is doing God's will, and anything that is the will of God has eternal significance.

True religion is to care for those who need help (James 1:27). Babies can't change their own diapers, so they must depend upon someone else to do it. The greatest in God's kingdom is the servant of all, and that includes serving infants. Because God is a Father who cares for the helpless, He will reward those who change diapers and care for children.

The Christian mother who changes her baby's diapers will be rewarded forever for performing that duty.

The Christian mechanic who repairs vehicles honestly, the farmer who toils long hours in the field, the butcher who works hard in the beef-packing plant, the clerk at the store who waits diligently on people, and the hard-working office secretary are all performing significant work in the kingdom of God.

How do I know? Because Abraham raised cattle for a living. Jacob raised sheep. They spent many days taking care of livestock in rural areas. Amos wasn't famous—he grew figs for a living. And God was pleased with their lives, even though no one knew who they were at the time.

Get a new perspective on your earthly occupation. Your vocation is a part of your calling in the kingdom of God. So whatever your job may be, start considering God your primary boss, and you will find eternal significance in your occupation.

Supporting Ministries
Jesus said:

> He who receives a prophet in the name of a prophet shall receive a prophet's reward; and he who receives a righteous man in the name of a righteous man shall receive a righteous man's reward. And whoever in the name of a disciple gives to one of these little ones even a cup of cold water to drink, truly I say to you, he shall not lose his reward. (Matthew 10:41–42)

When we support churches and ministries that are spreading the gospel of Jesus Christ, we will also share in their reward. Churches can't minister effectively without fellow workers who faithfully pray and give financial support. Intercessory prayer and encouraging those in full-time ministry are important ways that those who work secular jobs can become partners in their work.

God will even reward something as insignificant as giving a cup of cold water in His name. If He will reward us for giving away a cup of water, just think how He will bless us for giving away our lives.

Doing Good

> With good will render service, as to the Lord, and not to men, knowing that *whatever good thing each one does, this he will receive back from the Lord,* whether slave or free. (Ephesians 6:7–8)

God makes an incredible promise in this passage. He will personally reward us for every good deed we perform after we are born again. That's phenomenal, isn't it? If we help someone, speak a kind word, or go out of our way to meet a need or bless someone, God will reward us for each deed.

God gave us this information for a reason. Can you see how knowing this could change the way you treat people? Our ultimate motivation is to please God in all we do, and this promise helps us understand that our earthly actions have eternal purposes.

RANDOM ACTS OF RIGHTEOUSNESS

Here is a list of some things God will reward on Judgment Day—if they are performed out of love, kindness, and a pure heart toward God instead of for the reward.

- Witnessing to someone about Jesus (1 Corinthians 9:16–17)
- Leading someone to salvation (Proverbs 11:30)
- Being martyred for Christ (Hebrews 11:37)
- Seeking God diligently (Hebrews 11:6)
- Giving money for God's work (Matthew 6:3–4, 19–20)

- Praying (Matthew 6:6)
- Fasting (Matthew 6:17–18)
- Budgeting money wisely (Luke 16:11–12)
- Serving the Lord faithfully in ministry (Luke 19:17; 1 Corinthians 15:58)
- Helping others (Luke 6:35)
- Loving those who don't love in return (Matthew 5:46)
- Treating others with honor (Matthew 10:41)
- Being a godly spouse and parent (1 Peter 3:3–7)
- Working faithfully in earthly jobs (Colossians 3:22–24)
- Doing good deeds (Ephesians 6:7–8)
- Submitting with respect to unreasonable employers (1 Peter 2:18–20)
- Being persecuted for His name's sake (Luke 6:22–23)
- Having a servant's attitude (Mark 10:43–45)
- Humbling ourselves (Matthew 18:4)
- Doing little things for others (Matthew 10:42)
- Helping the poor (Proverbs 19:17)
- Visiting widows and orphans in their distress (James 1:27)
- Living righteously (Proverbs 11:31)

You probably won't make any headlines in earth's newspapers if you do the things on this list. But that's okay. Earth's newspapers are used to wrap dead fish. Heaven's headlines will be remembered forever.

MAKING THE MOST OF YOUR OPPORTUNITY

- Review each deed mentioned in this chapter, and evaluate your faithfulness in each area.
- Perform random acts of kindness. Start with your immediate family.
- Find a way to help someone anonymously.

chapter seven

THE FINAL EXAM

For we must all appear before the judgment seat of Christ,
so that each one may be recompensed for his deeds in the body,
according to what he has done, whether good or bad.

2 CORINTHIANS 5:10

When Rick Howard was in college, he walked into his classroom one day after having skipped class for nearly two weeks. He was ten minutes early, but every student was seated with books open, cramming for a test. His heart skipped a beat as he asked his friend, "What's up, Jim?"

Jim looked amused. "Oh, nothing special, Howard. Just the midsemester exam, that's all."

"You've got to be kidding!"

"Oh, no," Jim replied. "We do lots of exciting things here. You ought to come around here more often."

Rick approached his instructor and pleaded for a personal postponement of the test. His professor said, "Mr. Howard, I don't approve of this current attendance policy. I can't punish you for missing class, but you are nonetheless responsible for everything that goes on here. You must take the exam this morning with your fellow students or receive an automatic failure on this test."

Rick's heart sank to his stomach as he stared at the test, not knowing how to answer. He realized how foolish he had been for not having prepared for the exam.[1]

Are you ready for your final exam? Judgment Day is not an unannounced test. We must all appear before the judgment seat of Christ to give an account of things we have done. The judgment seat, or *bema* in Greek, is the place where we will receive our assignments for eternity.

Rick Howard, now an author, writes, "The judgment seat of Christ is the posting of the exam grades, the evaluation of our life's choices, and the establishment of our positions for eternity."[2]

After an athlete won an event at the Isthmian games in Corinth, he would proceed to the bema seat to receive his reward. Paul used this earthly event to demonstrate a heavenly truth. After we have finished running the race of life, we must appear at the bema seat in heaven to receive our rewards. This is why he encouraged us to "run in such a way that you may win" (1 Corinthians 9:24).

If God forgives our sins, why do we have to face the judgment? Weren't our sins judged on the cross? Yes. The judgment seat of Christ will not examine those sins. It will examine your works from the moment of salvation until death. God will demonstrate His grace and generosity on the day of rewards. His grace will be manifest because He saved us; His generosity will be shown when He rewards us.

CRAMMING

It always helps to know what's going to be on a test. How can you prepare properly if you don't know what's expected of you? God's final exam will cover three areas: our words, our motives, and our works.

1) God will judge us according to our words.
"But I tell you that every careless word that people speak, they shall give an accounting for it in the day of judgment" (Matthew 12:36). We will be held accountable on Judgment Day for everything we have said. Why? Because our words reveal what is in our hearts.

After concluding important negotiations with business leaders in his high-rise office building, John D. Rockefeller used to say good-bye to his visitors at the elevator. As the visitors filed into the elevator, an innocent looking man would slip in and ride with them to the ground floor. He would follow the group out the door and then cross the street. A few minutes later, he would return to Rockefeller's office to deliver a detailed report on what the unsuspecting visitors had said in the elevator.[3]

What we say in private reveals our true feelings. The words spoken in secret will one day be made known to everyone. Jesus said:

> "There is nothing covered up that will not be revealed, and hidden that will not be known. Accordingly, whatever you have said in the dark will be heard in the light, and what you have whispered in the inner rooms will be proclaimed upon the housetops." (Luke 12:2–3)

Words spoken for edification will be rewarded, but unwholesome words may cause some people to lose rewards.

2) God will judge us according to our motives.
God not only sees what we do, but also examines our motives.

> Therefore do not go on passing judgment before the time, but wait until the Lord comes who will both bring to light the things hidden in the darkness and *disclose the motives of men's hearts;* and then each man's praise will come to him from God. (1 Corinthians 4:5)

If the devil can't get us to do wrong, he will tempt us to do right for the wrong reasons. The Pharisees diligently performed the right duties by giving money, praying, and fasting. Although those deeds were good, their motives were evil. These self-made religious zealots were gloating givers, professional prayers, and fanatical fasters. They craved admiration from men but not from God. Jesus said that their selfish motives canceled out their rewards (Matthew 6:2, 5).

May I ask you a personal question? If you are serving the Lord, *why* are you doing it? Is it out of obligation? Has someone pressured you to do it? Is it because you'll feel guilty if you don't? Do you want others to see you do it so they'll admire you?

All of these motives are wrong. God wants us to serve Him out of a heart that burns with love for Him. When we desire to make God smile, our motives will always be right.

3) God will judge us according to our works.
God will examine all our works and reward what pleases Him. "For God is not unjust so as to forget your work and the love which you have shown toward His name, in having ministered and in still min-

istering to the saints" (Hebrews 6:10). On the Day of judgment, God will separate our good and bad works to determine our reward.

> Now if any man builds on the foundation with gold, silver, precious stones, wood, hay, straw, each man's work will become evident; for the day will show it because it is to be revealed with fire, and the fire itself will test the quality of each man's work. If any man's work which he has built on it remains, he will receive a reward. (1 Corinthians 3:12–14)

The foundation is the most important stage of construction. Everything else is built upon it. A house with a faulty foundation is destined for an inevitable collapse (Matthew 7:26).

Some people build on the shaky foundation of self-sufficiency. Others structure their lives on worldly success, sexual pleasure, or false religions. When we accept Jesus Christ as Lord and Savior, He becomes the sure foundation on which we build our lives. Without Him as our foundation, all our works will come tumbling down.

Once the foundation is laid, we spend the rest of our lives building on it. Peter tells us to "live *the rest of the time in the flesh* no longer for the lusts of men, but for the will of God" (1 Peter 4:2). The "rest of the time" is our remaining years of life on earth. The construction materials represent the way we live after we are saved because we build *upon* the foundation. God's grace not only lays the foundation, but also gives us the desire and power to build upon it.

The materials, our postconversion deeds, fall into two categories. The gold, silver, and precious stones are those activities mentioned in the previous chapter—deeds that demonstrate our love for God. These will be rewarded throughout our eternal existence. The wood, hay, and straw are our selfish deeds and attitudes that won't be rewarded and could even cause a loss of reward.

Wood, Hay, Straw	Gold, Silver, Precious Stones
Disobedience and selfish motives	Doing things for God's glory
Wasting money on useless items	Cheerfully giving money to God
Causing division and strife	Teaching Sunday school or Bible study
Gossiping about others	Praying for others
Manipulating others	Serving others
Criticizing others	Being persecuted for righteousness sake
Laziness	Faithful work

Some people believe that everyone in heaven will have equal rewards because we are all saved by God's grace. I respectfully disagree. While it is true that salvation is a gift that can't be earned, rewards are bonuses bestowed for faithful service. God lets us decide how we will build on the foundation, and He will reward us accordingly. This unique opportunity to build with gold, silver, and precious stones is available to all who wish to dedicate their lives to the glory of God.

KINDLING

Since we are rewarded for godly deeds, will we lose rewards for the evil things we have done? Paul gives us the answer:

We must all appear before the judgment seat of Christ, so that each one may be recompensed for his deeds in the body, according to what he has done, *whether good or bad.* (2 Corinthians 5:10)

Bad deeds will not be judged as sins, but as the wood, hay, and straw that will be burned up (1 Corinthians 3:12). On that day fire will test the believer's works, not the believer himself. "If any man's work is burned up, he will suffer loss; but he himself will be saved, yet so as through fire" (v. 15).

Imagine a man who spends his entire life constructing a house. When he is finished, he goes inside, and the house catches fire. Fortunately, he is able to escape his flaming house. Although the builder survives, his work is burned up.

Some Christians spend their entire lives on earth building with wood, hay, and straw. When the flame comes to test the quality of their works, all their deeds will be destroyed. They will be admitted into heaven but will be saved "as through fire." They will forfeit rewards they could have enjoyed.

After spending months writing his book *The French Revolution,* Thomas Carlyle took his manuscript to his friend John Stuart Mill for his comments. Mill passed on the manuscript to a lady named Mrs. Chapman, who read it by the fireplace on the evening of March 5, 1834. Before she went to bed that night, she laid the manuscript on the mantel.

Early the next morning the servant girl came to clean the room and start a fire in the fireplace. Not knowing what the papers were, she used the manuscript to kindle the fire. The work of months was burned up in a matter of seconds.

At the judgment seat of Christ, many people's work will also go up in flames. Probably everyone will have at least some work burned up. Haven't you ever done anything selfish? Say good-bye to it. Bitterness, complaining, and evil behavior will probably result in the loss of rewards. "Watch yourselves, that you do not lose what we have accomplished, but that you may receive *a full reward*" (2 John 1:8).

Although many will lose rewards, God Himself will richly reward those who have built with gold, silver, and precious stones.

CROWNING

Some people will receive crowns as a special reward for living sacrificially on earth. The twenty-four elders seated around God's throne wear golden crowns and white garments (Revelation 4:4). While we don't know exactly what these crowns represent or who these individuals are, we do know that these people overcame intense difficulties. The Greek word used for *crown* in this passage is *stephanos,* which means a victor's crown.

Five different crowns are mentioned in Scripture:

- the *imperishable crown* for those who lead disciplined lives (1 Corinthians 9:25–27);
- the *crown of rejoicing* for those who lead others to Christ (1 Thessalonians 2:19–20; Philippians 4:1);
- the *crown of righteousness* for those who love His appearing (2 Timothy 4:8);
- the *crown of glory* for those who faithfully shepherd the flock (1 Peter 5:2–4);
- the *crown of life* for those who overcome spiritual battles (James 1:12; Revelation 2:10).

Because pride doesn't exist in heaven, these crowns won't be awarded so we can show off our earthly accomplishments. Nor will they be to make a fashion statement. I think that these unique rewards most likely signify our positions and assignments in heaven.

The list of crowns is probably more suggestive than it is exhaustive. God may hand out crowns to faithful believers for other reasons. I bet that He has many surprises in store for us. Perhaps the biggest surprise is that God can find anything in us worth rewarding. It just goes to show what a merciful and generous God we serve.

There's a final exam coming. It's no pop quiz, but many will not be ready for it when it comes. Begin today to eliminate the worthless wood, hay, and straw deeds from your life and to maximize the deeds of gold, silver, and precious stones.

Making the Most of Your Opportunity

- How do you talk about others? Find ways to speak positively instead of negatively.
- Take an honest look inside your heart and examine your motives. What do you see? Make the necessary corrections.

chapter eight

GRADUATION DAY

You will be repaid at the resurrection of the righteous.

LUKE 14:14

B aron de Rothschild was one of the richest men who had ever lived. One day he decided that it would be humorous to dress up like a beggar and have his portrait painted by an artist named Ary Scheffer. The Baron put on rags, struck a pose, and held out a tin cup. While he was posing, a friend of the artist entered the room. Thinking he was a real beggar, the friend dropped a coin into Rothschild's tin cup.

Ten years later, the man who had given the money to Rothschild received a letter containing a bank order for ten thousand francs. The note said, "Years ago you gave some money to a beggar in the studio of Ary Scheffer. Today he sends you the returns on your investment. Signed, Baron de Rothschild."[1]

Have you ever loaned money to someone who never repaid

you? Jesus told us that when we lend and expect nothing in return, our reward will be great (Luke 6:35). Do you believe that God will repay you in the future? If so, then there's no need to be angry with anyone who owes you.

God will repay all debts and compensate His children for their giving and good deeds on Graduation Day, the resurrection of the righteous. At the time we receive our resurrection bodies, we will also receive our eternal rewards and assignments for the next life.

GUESS WHO'S COMING TO DINNER?

So what does having a banquet have to do with the resurrection and rewards? Do you mean to tell me that reaching out to society's down-and-outers will make a difference in my eternal future? That's what Jesus said.

> "When you give a luncheon or a dinner, do not invite your friends or your brothers or your relatives or rich neighbors, otherwise they may also invite you in return and that will be your repayment.... Invite the poor, the crippled, the lame, the blind, and you will be blessed...for you will be repaid at the resurrection of the righteous." (Luke 14:12–14)

We naturally want to invite friends, relatives, and the wealthy. There's nothing wrong with that. But Jesus said that if you want to be blessed on Resurrection Day, go a step further. Change the address labels and invite the disabled and poverty-stricken.

Let's pretend for a moment that we're actually going to throw this party. When the crippled, lame, and blind arrive at the dinner, we will have to help feed them because they probably won't be able to feed themselves. The blind and crippled may need some assistance getting around. Afterwards we'll probably be financially strapped for a while. These people can't repay us, so we must wait until a future day to be reimbursed.

But the real party doesn't begin for a while. Jesus said that when we give to those who can't pay us back, God will repay us at the resurrection of the righteous—the ultimate celebration. That's one party that will literally last forever. And the formerly crippled, lame, and blind you invited to dinner will rejoice with you in their perfected resurrection bodies.

Although many people talk about going to heaven, few understand the importance of Resurrection Day. Paul eagerly looked forward to it. He said, "In the future there is laid up for me the crown of righteousness, which the Lord, the righteous Judge, will award to me on that day; and not only to me, but also to all who have loved His appearing" (2 Timothy 4:8).

Jesus said, "I am the resurrection and the life; he who believes in Me will live even if he dies" (John 11:25). His resurrection guarantees that everyone who believes in Him will be raised in the resurrection of the righteous.

Jesus said that there will be two different kinds of resurrections:

"Do not marvel at this; for an hour is coming, in which all who are in the tombs will hear His voice, and will come forth; those who did the good deeds to a resurrection of life, those who committed the evil deeds to a resurrection of judgment." (John 5:28–29)

One way or another, all who have ever lived on earth will be raised from the dead. They will either be raised in the resurrection of life or in the resurrection of judgment.

QUESTIONS ABOUT THE RESURRECTION

I'm sure you have wondered, as I have, how God will resurrect people out of dirt. Sure, I believe in the Resurrection with all my heart. I just haven't figured out how God will put all those molecules back together again. The Corinthians asked the same questions about this subject that many people ask today.

Question #1: "How are the dead raised?" (1 Corinthians 15:35)
The Lord told Adam:

> "By the sweat of your face
>   You will eat bread,
> Till you return to the ground,
>   Because from it you were taken;
> For you are dust,
>   And to dust you shall return." (Genesis 3:19)

God created Adam out of the dust of the ground. Eventually his body deteriorated back to dust. How is it possible to reconstruct people from dust?

We might find it easy to believe that Jesus was resurrected because all His "parts" were still attached. Although He had been dead for three days, He hadn't disintegrated into dust like someone who has been dead for three thousand years.

I have finally come to this realization: If someone can explain to me how God constructed man out of dust in the first place, I will tell you how He will reconstruct us out of it. To put together someone who has disintegrated might be a problem for us, but not for God. Since God created Adam from dirt, He won't have a problem reassembling the dead from it.

The resurrection of our bodies does not depend upon us understanding how God will do it. When we grasp the fact that nothing is impossible with God, resurrection becomes simple. Absolutely nothing, including raising the dead, is too difficult for God (Jeremiah 32:17). God created the universe out of nothing, so resurrecting people out of dust is minor league for Him (Hebrews 11:3).

Question #2: "With what kind of body do they come?"
(1 Corinthians 15:35)

God will give us the resurrection bodies He has decided upon (1 Corinthians 15:38). When a seed is buried in the ground, a plant—not another seed—comes out of the seed. The plant doesn't look like the seed it came from. When we are buried in the ground and resurrected, our bodies won't look identical to the ones we have now.

"All flesh is not the same flesh, but there is one flesh of men, and another flesh of beasts, and another flesh of birds, and another of fish" (1 Corinthians 15:39). The flesh of men is made for walking, that of birds for flying, and that of fish for swimming. God designs bodies to fit the environment they will live in.

Our resurrection bodies will be perfect for the environment of heaven. Earthly bodies equip us to live on earth. We breathe the earth's oxygen, drink its water, and eat its fruit. However, these earthly bodies aren't suitable for heaven. To get us ready for the next world, they must undergo a change. We must go through a transformation process that will make us like the angels in heaven (Matthew 22:30). We won't *be* angels, but we will be like them in that we will have similar bodies.

THE TRANSFORMATION PROCESS

Your present body was created to last only a few years. Your resurrection body will equip you for a much higher level of existence. Paul contrasted the differences between them:

> So also is the resurrection of the dead. It is sown a perishable body, it is raised an imperishable body; it is sown in dishonor, it is raised in glory; it is sown in weakness, it is raised in power; it is sown a natural body, it is raised a spiritual body. (1 Corinthians 15:42–44)

This chart compares the differences between the earthly and resurrection body.

EARTHLY BODY	RESURRECTION BODY
Sown a perishable body *(1 Corinthians 15:42)*	Raised an imperishable body *(1 Corinthians 15:42)*
Sown in dishonor *(1 Corinthians 15:43)*	Raised in glory *(1 Corinthians 15:43)*
Sown in weakness *(1 Corinthians 15:43)*	Raised in power *(1 Corinthians 15:43)*
Sown a natural body *(1 Corinthians 15:44)*	Raised a spiritual body *(1 Corinthians 15:44)*

At the resurrection, our bodies will be transformed from our current "caterpillar" form to our future "butterfly" status. The beauty of a butterfly is far superior to that of a caterpillar, but the butterfly has to go through the transformation process first.

Four changes must take place to transform your body from earthly to heavenly.

Change #1: Perishable to Imperishable

Our present bodies are perishable, and they degenerate as we race toward the grave. Just like Adam, we are headed back to dust. In the resurrection, however, we will be raised imperishable—never to deteriorate or die again.

Sir Michael Faraday, one of England's greatest chemists and physicists, reportedly heard a student scoff at the idea of the resurrection. Faraday threw a silver goblet into a jar of acid, which completely dissolved it. He then added other chemicals that caused the silver to settle to the bottom of the jar. The chemist then took the silver to a silversmith, who made it into a goblet more beautiful than the first.

Then Faraday held up the goblet and told the student, "If I, an ordinary scientist, can dissolve and remake a silver goblet, why is it hard to believe that God can raise the body from the dead?"[2]

God will transform your perishable body into one that is indestructible. Once you receive it, dying will be impossible. You will live in it throughout eternity.

Change #2: Dishonor to Glory

What's there to celebrate about a rotting corpse? Absolutely nothing. But God promises that we will be raised in glory. Jesus looked different after He rose from the dead:

His head and His hair were white like white wool, like snow; and His eyes were like a flame of fire. His feet were like burnished bronze, when it has been made to glow in a furnace…. And His face was like the sun shining in its strength. (Revelation 1:14–16)

There's a huge difference in brightness between a twenty-five-watt lightbulb and a thousand-watt bulb. In the resurrection, our "lumens" of brightness will be turned up to the fullest. Our resurrection bodies will literally shine with brightness, just like Jesus'. "THE RIGHTEOUS WILL *SHINE FORTH AS THE SUN* in the kingdom of their Father" (Matthew 13:43). The prophet Daniel described the appearance of our resurrected bodies:

"Those who have insight *will shine brightly like the brightness of the expanse of heaven,* and those who lead the many to righteousness, *like the stars forever and ever."* (Daniel 12:3)

And Paul said:

There are also heavenly bodies and earthly bodies, but the glory of the heavenly is one, and the glory of the earthly is another. There is one glory of the sun, and another glory of the moon, and another glory of the stars; for star differs from star in glory. (1 Corinthians 15:40–41)

This passage could mean that there will be differing degrees of brightness in our glorified bodies. Or perhaps it refers to the difference in glory between our natural and resurrection bodies. One thing is certain: Every resurrection body will be without defect and will literally radiate brightness.

Change #3: Weakness to Power

Our resurrection bodies will be extremely powerful. We will never grow weary or weak. Can you imagine not having to sleep throughout all eternity? Since there will be no need to nap, we will never again have to toss and turn on lumpy mattresses. Wives will not have to listen to husbands' snoring anymore. No more insomnia, sleeping pills, or alarm clocks, either. Our way of life will be radically different than our lifestyles here on earth.

When Jesus rose from the dead, He could appear and disappear at will and ascend into heaven. If for some reason in eternity we needed to travel through space, we could easily do so. We will not be limited as we are in our present bodies.

Scripture indicates that in eternity we will comprehend things that we can't now. We will all see Jesus personally, face-to-face (1 Corinthians 13:12). As we stand in His presence, we will understand the answers to the nagging questions that bugged us in this life.

The Bible also hints that resurrected people will be able to eat in eternity. Since we will have glorified taste buds, I'm confident that every bite will be heavenly. Apparently we will eat from the tree of life, which will bear twelve kinds of fruit (Revelation 22:2). The leaves from the tree of life are for the healing of the nations.

We will understand the answers to the nagging questions that bugged us in this life.

Obviously, resurrection bodies won't need to be healed. The Greek word behind *healing* is *therapeian*, from which we get the

English word *therapeutic*. Rather than specifically meaning *healing,* in this case it should be understood to mean *health giving.* In other words, the leaves of the tree promote the enjoyment of life in the new Jerusalem and are not for correcting ills, which do not exist. This is confirmed by the fact that there is no more curse (Revelation 22:3).[3]

You will sit down and dine with those you've read about in the Bible. "I say to you that many will come from east and west, and *recline at the table* with Abraham, Isaac and Jacob in the kingdom of heaven" (Matthew 8:11). If you are a Christian, you are reading about yourself in this passage. You are one of the many who will come from the east and the west to dine with the resurrected prophets of old.

Won't it be great to meet Moses and hear him explain how God split the Red Sea? You'll get to personally interview David, who will tell you how he pitched a one-hitter against Goliath. I'm looking forward to hearing Jonah tell how he took a submarine ride and was torpedoed onto shore. Peter will laugh as he explains to you how he walked on the water, and then sank.

And, of course, we will be glad to be reunited with loved ones who have gone on before us. We will literally meet all the people who have been redeemed throughout the history of the earth, and we will hear their stories. What an exciting time that will be!

Change #4: Natural to Spiritual

Our resurrection bodies will be spiritual. This refers to the *kind* of body we will have. When the disciples saw Jesus after He was resurrected, they thought they had seen a spirit. Jesus told them, "A spirit does not have flesh and bones as you see that I have" (Luke 24:39). Jesus did not become a spirit, but was raised with a spiritual body. In heaven we will not be "spirits," but we will have spiritual bodies.

After Jesus died and rose from the dead, He didn't have two bodies, one natural and another spiritual. He had only one body—a natural body that had been transformed into a spiritual body. Jesus showed His disciples the marks of the nails in His hands and feet and the wound in His side, which proved that it was the same body. But that body had undergone a radical change. When you are resurrected, your body also will be changed and perfected.

A sedimentary rock that is subjected to heat and pressure becomes a metamorphic rock. It's the same rock, but it has undergone a change. In the same way, your resurrection body will be the same one you have now, but it will have gone through a transformation. The spiritual body is derived from the natural body. This is why we must live in our earthly bodies first: "The spiritual is not first, but the natural; then the spiritual" (1 Corinthians 15:46).

AFTER GRADUATION

Do you recognize a pattern here? Let's do a quick review.

The Test—*our time on earth.*
The Final Exam—*the judgment seat of Christ.*
Graduation Day—*a new era begins. Celebrate!*

After graduating, you've got to find a job. Fortunately, heaven's placement office has a perfect assignment awaiting you in God's eternal kingdom. Next we'll take a look at what you can expect to find in your eternal place of residence.

Making the Most of Your Opportunity

- Invite an impaired or lonely person over to your house to eat.
- This week help at least three people who can't repay you.

chapter nine

HAPPILY EVER AFTER

*"He will wipe away every tear from their eyes;
and there will no longer be any death;
there will no longer be any mourning, or crying, or pain;
the first things have passed away."*

REVELATION 21:4

When William Montague Dyke was ten years old, he was blinded in an accident. Despite his disability, William graduated from a university in England with high honors. While he was in school, he fell in love with the daughter of a high-ranking British naval officer, and they became engaged.

Not long before the wedding, William had eye surgery in the hope that the operation would restore his sight. If it failed, he would remain blind for the rest of his life. William insisted on keeping the bandages on his face until his wedding day. If the surgery had been successful, he wanted the first person he saw to be his new bride.

The wedding day arrived. The many guests—including royalty, cabinet members, and distinguished men and women of society—assembled to witness the exchange of vows. William's father, Sir William Hart Dyke, and the doctor who performed the surgery stood next to the groom, whose eyes were still covered with bandages. The organ trumpeted the wedding march, and the bride slowly walked down the aisle to the front of the church.

As soon as she arrived at the altar, the surgeon took a pair of scissors out of his pocket and cut the bandages from William's eyes.

Tension filled the room. The congregation of witnesses held their breath as they waited to find out if William could see the woman standing before him. As he stood face-to-face with his bride-to-be, William's words echoed throughout the cathedral, "You are more beautiful than I ever imagined!"

FUTURE WEDDING

One day the bandages that cover *our* eyes will be removed. When we stand face-to-face with Jesus Christ and see His face for the very first time, His glory will be far more splendid than anything we have ever imagined in this life. I'm anxious to see the God who made us and saved us, aren't you?

It's far better to be with Jesus in heaven than to remain here on earth (Philippians 1:23). Christians don't have to be afraid of dying. We can look forward to being with Christ forever. God assures every believer that heaven is a place where His children will live happily ever after.

What will heaven be like? Although God hasn't given us the entire picture, He has revealed a few pieces of the puzzle. Let's do some detective work and examine some passages that will help solve the mystery.

The New Earth

Peter gives us a clue about what will happen in the next life:

> The heavens will pass away with a roar and the elements
> will be destroyed with intense heat, and the earth and its
> works will be burned up.... But according to His promise
> we are looking for new heavens and a new earth, in which
> righteousness dwells. (2 Peter 3:10, 13)

Why will God do away with this world and create something
entirely new? Why doesn't He just salvage the useful parts and
make a few repairs to this old, worn-out planet?

This present order of things must pass away for God to bring
about His new creation. God will destroy the earth by fire because
it will have served its purpose. He created it as a temporary world
so that He could choose a people for His own possession (Titus
2:14; 1 Peter 2:9). When He has chosen His forever family, He can
create a new earth for them that will never be destroyed.

That which God redeemed in His first creation will be transformed into His next creation. Our natural bodies will be changed
into resurrection bodies. Heavenly assignments will replace earthly
jobs. God will even give us new names (Revelation 2:17). God will
speak to us personally, calling us by these new names. Our magnificent Lord, who whirled the galaxies into existence and numbers
the hairs on our heads, still cares deeply for us as individuals.

God will remove all pain and suffering by taking His eternal
Kleenex and personally wiping away all tears from our eyes. Our
worst nightmares will be behind us, and our greatest adventures
will lie before us in God's eternal kingdom.

No one will long for the "good old days" on earth, for they will
seem trivial compared to the splendor of heaven:

"For behold, I create new heavens and a new earth;
And *the former things will not be remembered or come to mind.*" (Isaiah 65:17)

This doesn't mean that we'll have no memory of our earthly existence. It's just that the blessings of heaven will be so wonderful that they will far outshine our most exciting times on earth. What has been the most exciting time of your life up until now? It will be dull and boring compared to what you will experience in heaven.

Our worst nightmares will be behind us, and our greatest adventures will lie before us in God's eternal kingdom.

The New Jerusalem

The apostle John gives us the next clue about the future. After the new earth is created, the new Jerusalem will be transferred from heaven to earth. "And I saw the holy city, new Jerusalem, coming down out of heaven from God" (Revelation 21:2). The city is not heaven itself, because it comes down out of heaven (Revelation 3:12; 21:2, 10). The new Jerusalem, the capital of the new earth, is described as a cube of fifteen hundred miles long, wide, and high, or about half the area of the United States. Because the city is fifteen hundred miles high, some people believe it will be structured in stories, one layer upon another.

The heavenly city is called by several names:

- the new Jerusalem (Revelation 3:12; 21:2)
- the holy city (Revelation 21:2; 22:19)
- the Jerusalem above (Galatians 4:26)

- the city whose architect and builder is God (Hebrews 11:10)
- the city that God has prepared (Hebrews 11:16)
- the heavenly Jerusalem (Hebrews 12:22)
- the city of the living God (Hebrews 12:22)
- the city that is to come (Hebrews 13:14)
- My Father's house (John 14:1–3)

Is the new Jerusalem a real city or merely a symbol? Some people believe it is symbolic because Jesus speaks of making us pillars in the temple (Revelation 3:12). While it is true that much of the book of Revelation is symbolic, I believe the above Scriptures support the conclusion that this is indeed a literal city.

Thousands of years ago, Abraham "was looking for the city which has foundations, whose architect and builder is God" (Hebrews 11:10). The writer of Hebrews exhorts us, "For here we do not have a lasting city, but we are seeking the city which is to come" (Hebrews 13:14). God has prepared this heavenly city for all who love Him. "But as it is, they desire a better country, that is, a heavenly one. Therefore God is not ashamed to be called their God; for He has prepared a city for them" (Hebrews 11:16). Jesus said that in His Father's house are many dwelling places, or rooms, which He has prepared for His followers (John 14:1–3).

Let's take a walk around the city, shall we? The new Jerusalem is surrounded by a wall with twelve gates, with the names of the twelve tribes of Israel written on each gate. Revelation 21:21 tells us that each gate is a single pearl. (Can you imagine the size of the oysters?)

Notice that the wall has twelve foundation stones, and on each stone is a name of one of the twelve apostles. The Old Testament age is represented by names of the twelve tribes on the gates, while the New Testament era is represented by names of the twelve apostles on the foundation stones. Both Old and New Testament believers will dwell in the heavenly city.

Brilliant light radiates from the new Jerusalem because the glory of God is its light source. The glow of the city illuminates the entire planet. "And the city has no need of the sun or of the moon to shine on it, for the glory of God has illumined it, and its lamp is the Lamb. The *nations will walk by its light*" (Revelation 21:23–24). Won't it be nice not having to pay electric bills or change lightbulbs anymore?

The details about eternity are hazy at best, but let me tell you what I believe will occur. The redeemed people from all periods of history will be the citizens of the new earth. Although all of us will have a dwelling place in the new Jerusalem, we will have responsibilities on the new earth outside the city. Evidently, lots of traffic will go in and out of the city, to and from the new earth. I believe that people will have assignments in different areas of the new earth, which will be divided into nations.

There will not only be nations on the new earth, but also kings. "The kings of the earth will bring their glory into it" (Revelation 21:24). Who are these kings who enter the city? Let's speculate a little further. Kings are the highest authorities in countries, so these kings probably hold the highest positions in the nations on the new earth. No doubt they represent the most faithful servants of the Lord from this present earth. Jesus said, "He who overcomes, and he who keeps My deeds until the end, TO HIM I WILL GIVE *AUTHORITY OVER THE NATIONS*" (Revelation 2:26).

In this future kingdom of God, some people will be selected to rule in these high positions as kings. Didn't Jesus say that those who humble themselves will be exalted (Luke 14:11)? Several times He told us that the last will be first and that servants and slaves will be great in His kingdom. He also taught that if we are faithful with a few things, He will put us in charge of many things.

Is it possible that our duties will extend to the nations and cities on the new earth? If this is the case, those who faithfully served God during their lives on earth will be promoted to rule over nations, while others will be given authority over cities.

Remember the parable of the minas? The faithful slaves were rewarded by being placed in authority over cities. After the master received a kingdom for himself, he put one slave in charge of ten cities and another in charge of five cities. Could it be that Jesus actually meant literal cities—not on this present earth, but on the new earth? Slaves in those days were never put in charge of cities, so it's possible that Jesus was referring to future responsibilities in the kingdom of God.

I'm not trying to form a doctrine based on so few facts, but I find it fascinating to speculate about how all the pieces fit in this gigantic, eternal puzzle.

Erwin Lutzer writes:

> Christ told a parable that taught that the faithful were given authority over cities. Most scholars believe that will be fulfilled during the millennial kingdom when we shall rule with Christ here on earth. But it is reasonable to assume that there is continuity between the earthly kingdom and the eternal heavenly kingdom. In other words, it may well be that our faithfulness (or unfaithfulness) on earth may have repercussions throughout eternity. Just as there are varied responsibilities in the palace of an earthly king, so in heaven some will be given more prominent responsibilities than others.[1]

So what will the kingdom of God look like when we work all of this into a composite sketch? Maybe something like this: God will set up a government composed of different ranks and positions. Nations will cover the earth, with kings in authority over each one. Jesus will be the "KING OF KINGS AND LORD OF LORDS" throughout eternity (Revelation 19:16). Positions throughout the kingdom, from least to greatest, will be assigned according to how faithfully we lived on earth, our Opportunity. Although we will have different duties and assignments, everyone in heaven will be totally fulfilled as we worship and serve King Jesus together.

Eternal Dwellings

Remember how God uses some objects on earth to teach us about things in heaven? Jesus said, "If I told you earthly things and you do not believe, how will you believe if I tell you heavenly things?" (John 3:12). I am persuaded that our earthly homes give us a hint about what lies ahead for us in heaven.

Jesus compared our temporary houses on earth with eternal dwellings in heaven in the parable of the unjust steward (Luke 16:1–9). His conclusion:

> "I tell you, use worldly wealth to gain friends for your-selves, so that when it is gone, *you will be welcomed into eternal dwellings.*" (Luke 16:9, NIV)

What are these eternal dwellings? Will they be heavenly houses similar to here on earth? Well, let's think about that.

Will they have bedrooms? Since our resurrected bodies will never get tired, we won't need to sleep. Not even afternoon naps. Let's not lose sleep worrying about bedrooms.

What about bathrooms? I can't imagine that this room will ever be needed in heaven. Eliminate this one.

Kitchens? We know that the tree of life produces twelve kinds of fruit (Revelation 22:2), so I'm sure the recipes would be endless. But it's just hard to see myself stir-frying fruit from the tree of life. Heavenly produce needs no seasoning or improvements. Let's scrap kitchens from the blueprints.

How about a garage? The streets of gold must be used for something. But why would we want to drive when we could just fly wherever we want to go? Cars in heaven? Traffic lights? Speeding tickets? Pollution? Heaven forbid. It's safe to say we won't need garages in our eternal dwellings.

Living room or dining room? Jesus said we would recline at the table with Abraham, Isaac, and Jacob (Matthew 8:11). But if this is all we need the house for, couldn't we just have a picnic table outside? We will have no need for a roof on the house because it won't rain or snow or hail. The weather will always be perfect for our picnics with the prophets.

Just as earthly homes serve

an earthly purpose,

our eternal dwellings

will serve a heavenly purpose.

What then are these eternal dwellings? Good question. Although Jesus gave us a clue that something much grander exists in heaven, He didn't reveal all the specifics about eternity. Are they literal structures? I believe so. Jesus said, "In My Father's house are many dwelling places; *if it were not so, I would have told you; for I go to prepare a place for you*" (John 14:2).

But as to what we will use them for, we'll just have to wait and see. Just as earthly homes serve an earthly purpose, our eternal dwellings will serve a heavenly purpose. We won't comprehend their function until we get there.

Marriages in Heaven?

An engaged couple met untimely deaths. When they arrived in heaven, they asked God for permission to marry. The Lord said, "It's a bit unusual, but wait five years to see if you still want to marry each other."

Five years passed, and they made their request again. God said, "I want you to wait another five years." After waiting ten years, they finally received permission and were married. It wasn't long before they realized they had made a horrible mistake, and they asked God for a divorce.

The Lord said, "Look, it took us ten years to find a minister here. Do you realize how long it will take to find a lawyer?"

In heaven there will be people who were ministers and lawyers on earth, but there won't be marriage or divorce. The institution of marriage was designed for this earthly life only. Jesus said:

> "The sons of *this age* marry and are given in marriage, but those who are considered worthy to attain to *that age* and the resurrection from the dead, neither marry nor are given in marriage; for they cannot even die anymore, because they are like angels, and are sons of God, being sons of the resurrection." (Luke 20:34–36)

Since marriages won't exist in heaven, no children will be born in the next life. Those who were husband and wife on earth will know each other in heaven, but they won't be married, since the marriage covenant is dissolved when a person dies (Romans 7:2).

Although this saddens me, I always remind myself that everything in heaven is far better than anything on earth. Did God make a mistake by not including marriage in the next life? Certainly not. No one will be disappointed in heaven, and *all* relationships will be exalted to perfection in God's eternal kingdom.

Worship in Eternity

What will worship be like in heaven? Revelation 4:10 says, "The twenty-four elders will fall down before Him who sits on the throne, and will worship Him who lives forever and ever, and will cast their crowns before the throne."

Remember our list of crowns that God will award? These crowns are not to honor the people who received them, but the One who bestowed them. The twenty-four elders glorify Jesus by casting their crowns before His throne (Revelation 4:10). As an act of their worship, they return the very crowns the Lord awarded them to their King. The greater the reward we receive in heaven, the better our ability to honor and worship our Lord.

We will worship and serve the Lord throughout all eternity. Whatever we worship, we also serve. "For this reason, they are *before the throne* of God; and they *serve Him* day and night in His temple" (Revelation 7:15).

Worship in heaven will be pure ecstasy. Imagine praising our Lord forever! You don't have to wait until heaven to start worshiping with excitement and joy. Since God desires His will to be done on earth as it is in heaven (Matthew 6:10), you have His permission to start rejoicing at this very moment. Our worship and praise on earth is a practice session for what we will experience forever.

Job Assignments

Work in heaven? You thought you'd finally be free from work, didn't you? But work itself is not a result of the Fall. When the world was a paradise, God gave Adam the job of taking care of the Garden of Eden (Genesis 2:15). It wasn't until after Adam and Eve sinned that work became difficult and stressful (3:17–19). In heaven, the curse of misery and stress will be removed (Revelation 22:3). That means our jobs in eternity will be exciting and even fun, like our favorite hobbies.

Although the thought of working forever might not sound too thrilling, God wants us to look forward to these heavenly assignments. We would be bored stiff if we didn't have anything to do forever. Our resurrection bodies will be powerful and full of energy, so every task will be effortless. Work won't seem like work, but like recreation. Our jobs will be exhilarating and enjoyable, and they will fulfill our eternal calling.

We are not told what kind of service we will perform, but in our present state of knowledge, we couldn't understand it anyway. Suppose you perform a certain technical job in a factory and someone from a foreign country asks what you do for a living. Rather than explaining the specifics of your job, which he wouldn't understand, you simply say, "I work in a factory." The foreigner wouldn't understand much about your occupation, but he would have a vague idea of what you do.

God knows that we couldn't fathom the details of our eternal jobs, so He simply tells us that we will serve Him forever. Once we enter the eternal realm and our knowledge is expanded, we will understand. No doubt we will be performing millions of jobs, duties, responsibilities, and assignments, all with great excitement and purpose, from the ages unto the ages.

One thing we know for certain: Our assignments in heaven will be determined by how faithful we were to our earthly responsibilities.

Will Time Exist in Eternity?

Although some believe that time will not exist in eternity, others disagree. The much quoted verse "There should be time no longer" comes from the King James Version's rendering of Revelation 10:6. It actually means there will be no more *delay* before the next judgments come upon the earth during the Tribulation. Dr. John Walvoord commented on this verse:

> This expression (Greek, *chronos*) has sometimes been misunderstood to mean that time will cease. The expression here, however, does not refer to time as a succession of chronological events; rather it means that time has run out, that is, that there will be no further delay. Even in eternity, there will be a time relationship in that one event will follow another.[2]

There are several reasons to conclude that time will continue in heaven.

- Revelation 20:10 says that the devil, the beast, and the false prophet will be cast into the lake of fire and there be "tormented day and night forever and ever." The Greek words behind "forever and ever" literally mean "from age to age." An age is a period of time. Therefore it appears that eternity will be marked by a progressive series of time periods.
- Paul referred to our future when he said, "So that in the ages to come He might show the surpassing riches of His grace in kindness toward us in Christ Jesus" (Ephesians 2:7). He speaks not just of a future age, but of *ages* (plural). Daniel says, "But the saints of the Highest One will receive the kingdom and possess the kingdom forever, *for all ages to come*" (Daniel 7:18).

- God's people will serve Him around the clock throughout eternity: "For this reason, they are before the throne of God; and they serve Him *day and night* in His temple" (Revelation 7:15).
- The tree of life in the heavenly city will bear its fruit *every month* (Revelation 22:2). If time doesn't exist in eternity, why does God measure it in months?
- Some have suggested that God will create a new sun and moon, not as light sources, but as a way of tracking time:

"As the new heavens and the new earth that I make will endure before me," declares the LORD, "so will your name and descendants endure. *From one New Moon to another* and *from one Sabbath to another,* all mankind will come and bow down before me," says the LORD. (Isaiah 66:22–23, NIV)

- New Moons and Sabbaths would require a moon, a sun—and time. Time is God's way of separating events so that everything doesn't occur at once. "Then God said, 'Let there be lights in the expanse of the heavens to separate the day from the night, and let them be for signs and for seasons and for days and years'" (Genesis 1:14).

On the present earth we use the earth's rotation and revolution as a basis for time. Though we have no idea about the details about time on the new earth, if time does exist in eternity, it probably won't be as we now know it.

DO YOU HAVE RESERVATIONS?

What will our role be in the ages to come? Nothing short of mind-boggling! God has a plan mapped out for eternity future and offers us an incredible opportunity to be a part of it. I hope you've made your eternal reservations, for heaven's sake. If you have, like the ending of all good stories, you too will live happily ever after.

Making the Most of Your Opportunity

- Is heaven your future home? If you are unsure, read chapter 3 again.
- Start practicing for worship in heaven. Find a place to be alone and sing praises to God.

part three

Preparing for the Next Life

Don't be so heavenly minded that you are of no earthly good.
SATAN, THE FATHER OF LIES

Set your mind on things above, not on the things that are on earth.
THE APOSTLE PAUL, COLOSSIANS 3:2

Which of the above statements do you believe? I'll trust Paul over Satan any day. Contrary to popular opinion, being heavenly minded always inspires us to be of *more* earthly good.

You can still change your eternal destiny. By living to please your Lord and Savior, Jesus Christ, you can alter your future forever. In this section, you will learn how to properly prepare for your eternal home.

Many of the chapters concerning your next life are currently being written. It's up to you to fill in the pages. Being heavenly minded could make your final days on earth count forever. And that would make a great ending to your autobiography.

chapter ten

THE BIGGEST HEAD WON'T GET THE BIGGEST CROWN

"Everyone who exalts himself will be humbled,
and he who humbles himself will be exalted."

LUKE 14:11

Jesus said, "Whoever then humbles himself as this child, he is the greatest in the kingdom of heaven" (Matthew 18:4). Humility is the key to God's heart that unlocks His mercy. Sometimes we need a little help when it comes to removing pride, and, as in Paul's case, God is only too happy to help.

How would you like to have a grand tour of heaven but not be able to tell anyone what you saw? That's what happened to the apostle Paul. For some unknown reason, God chose to give Paul a preview of heaven, then sent him back to earth and told him to keep his mouth shut about what he had learned (2 Corinthians 12:2–4, 7).

Because of this remarkable revelation—not to mention his spectacular gifts and unparalleled calling—Paul could easily have gotten a big head. But the biggest crown won't go to the biggest head. To prevent Paul from getting overly impressed with himself, God gave him a thorn in the flesh, a messenger of Satan, to keep the swelling down (v. 7).

Think what would have happened if Paul hadn't received that thorn. Imagine Peter and Paul bumping into each other at the corner of Abraham Avenue and Lazarus Lane. Paul has just returned from his glorious trip to heaven but doesn't have the messenger of Satan to keep him humble. He might have acted something like this.

"Paul, where have you been? I've been looking for you everywhere."

"I just returned from an exclusive tour of heaven, Peter. God needed some advice on a few things, so I had to go up there to help Him out. Boy, was He glad to see me. I think He was about to make His first mistake."

"God showed you heaven?"

"That's right. Out of all the people in the entire world, God hand-picked me to see heaven. I suppose He could have chosen you, Peter, but He didn't want someone who opens his mouth only so he can change feet. I guess the fact that God chose me over you shows who He thinks is the most important apostle, doesn't it?"

"Well, I must admit I haven't had that experience yet. It's great that you got to go there. What did God tell you?"

"Oh, no, I can't tell you. That's just between God and me. It's our little secret. Sorry, Peter, but there are some things God and I can't reveal."

"Wow, Paul, that's amazing. Say, could we spend some time together? I haven't seen you in a while and—"

"I'd love to chat with you, Pete, but I've got more important things to do. Places to go, fans to meet, autographs to sign. Say hello to the little people back in Jerusalem for me, would you?"

God allowed Paul to have a thorn in the flesh to keep him from acting like this. The thorn's job was to burst his bubble whenever his ego started to inflate. Paul prayed three times for some heavenly tweezers to come down out of the sky to pluck out that thorn. But instead of removing it, God gave him thicker skin so he could endure it. Paul learned humility the hard way.

Humility means seeing ourselves realistically—as God sees us. Not higher than we are—but not lower, either. No matter how magnified we may look in this world, we are still microscopic when compared to God, and we need to be reminded continually of that fact. Without humility, we become proud and think that our abilities, looks, or resources come from ourselves instead of from God.

Because humility is the key characteristic God desires in His servants, we should do everything possible to embrace it. We won't be exalted in heaven without it.

The "Most Humble" Award

Do you know who was the most humble man in the Old Testament? Here's the answer: "Now the man Moses was very humble, more than any man who was on the face of the earth" (Numbers 12:3, written by Moses).

I'll bet it was hard for Moses to tell everyone that he was the most humble man on the face of earth. That's an honor he could be proud of.

A church realized the importance of humility, so it formed a committee to find the most humble person in the church. Many names were submitted and numerous candidates evaluated. Finally, the committee came to a unanimous decision. They selected a quiet little man who always lived in the background and had never taken credit for anything he had done. They awarded him the "Most Humble" button for his faithful service. However, the next day they had to take it away from him because he pinned it on.

Before we start removing people's "Most Humble" buttons, we need to clear up some misconceptions about humility. If we define humility in the wrong way, we will search for wrong ways to humble ourselves.

Humility does *not* mean that

- we should have low self-esteem or hate ourselves when we look in a mirror;
- we can't be promoted to a higher position. God promoted Joseph, Esther, and David to higher positions and used them there. Humility isn't determined by the position of our jobs, but the position of our hearts;
- we can't receive encouragement. If you are thanked, complimented, or encouraged for a job well done, kindly accept it and give the glory to God.

Now that we've had a crash course in humility, let's deal with its evil archenemy—pride. It's hard to detect conceit and arrogance in our lives until it is exposed. The following Humility Test is designed to reveal areas of pride in our hearts.

THE HUMILITY TEST

Check your answer in the box next to the question. No cheating. Dishonesty indicates that you are trying to hide pride.

Question #1: Have you become self-dependent instead of God-dependent? ❑ *Yes* ❑ *No*

One of the first indications that pride has slithered into our lives is when we are no longer dependent upon God. Whenever we think we can stand on our own, we are getting ready to fall (1 Corinthians 10:12).

A pastor was traveling on a bus down a bumpy road. Seated next to him was a college student who noticed that the minister was reading his Bible. The minister asked, "Are you spiritually ready for the temptations that you will face in college?"

"I don't have a problem with temptation," the young man told the minister. "I have strong willpower."

The minister took a pencil from his pocket and said, "I can make this pencil stand up on the cover of this Bible even though the bus ride is bumpy."

The young man said, "I'll believe it when I see it. I don't think you can do it."

"Look, I'm doing it," he replied as the young man watched.

"Yeah, but you didn't tell me you would hold the pencil up with your hand."

"I didn't have to tell you," the pastor remarked. "Have you ever seen a pencil stand up on its own without someone holding it?"

The minister then let go of the pencil, which instantly fell over. "The only reason you stand," he continued, "is because God is holding you up with His hand."

If God were to remove His hand of protecting grace, we would immediately fall into sin. Humility is depending completely on God, realizing that He upholds us by His grace (Romans 5:2).

*Question #2: Do you get upset when you don't receive recogni-
tion?* ❑ *Yes* ❑ *No*

God has chosen to accomplish much of His work on earth by using
people. Jesus indwells the bodies of all believers and wants to live
His life through us. Paul says that we are like clay pots used to hold
the precious treasure of God's Spirit (2 Corinthians 4:7). Our job as
pots is to empty ourselves so that the treasure, Jesus Christ, will be
glorified in our lives.

When God chooses to promote or use someone in an extraor-
dinary way, those who observe the person's remarkable talents in
the spotlight may misinterpret what is happening:

- they may give credit to the pot instead of the Treasure;
- they may exalt the messenger instead of the Message;
- they may honor the speaker instead of the Word;
- they may worship the singer instead of the Song.

Because God used him so mightily, Paul knew there was a danger that the honor people gave him could turn into pot worship.
Acts 14:8–18 records the story of how God used Paul and Barnabas
to heal a lame man. When the crowd observed the miracle, they
worshiped the clay pots instead of the Lord who did the healing.
And people have been worshiping the vessels that God uses ever
since! Through people worship we turn servants into celebrities.
Paul and Barnabas tried to correct the people's misdirected worship
by pointing them to the living God.

Pride loves to be worshiped. It craves attention and is greatly
offended when it is overlooked. Jesus asked the Pharisees, "How can
you believe, when you receive glory from one another and you do

not seek the glory that is from the one and only God?" (John 5:44). We can't give God the glory when we are seeking it for ourselves. It's not wrong to receive recognition or compliments, but it is wrong to seek after them. The humble person always desires to glorify God, not himself.

Pride loves to be worshiped and is greatly offended when it is overlooked.

One of the guests on a late-night talk show was a bodybuilder. The host asked the weightlifter if he would show off his muscles to the audience. With a big grin on his face, the bodybuilder faced the audience and cameras and flexed his muscles. "Boy," the host said, "you sure do have the muscles. What do you use all of those muscles for?" The bodybuilder didn't answer, but continued to flex and smile at the audience.

Again the host asked, "What *do* you use those muscles for?" Still grinning, the muscleman remained silent and continued to show off. The answer was obvious. He didn't use his muscles to do useful work, but only to glorify himself.

We can glorify ourselves in many different ways. We can use our looks, intelligence, job status, and personal accomplishments to glorify ourselves. We can even use our spiritual gifts and ministries to exalt ourselves instead of the God who gave us those gifts. When King Herod took for himself honor that rightly belonged to God, an angel struck him dead (Acts 12:23).

Humility recognizes that gifts and abilities come from God and that He therefore deserves all the credit.

Question #3: Do you think you deserve a higher position?
❑ *Yes* ❑ *No*

King Nebuchadnezzar reigned over the Babylonian Empire, which at that time ruled the ancient world. One day while he was walking on the roof of his royal palace, he said, "Is this not Babylon the great, which I myself have built as a royal residence by the might of my power and for the glory of my majesty?" (Daniel 4:30). The things we say reveal what's in our hearts.

> "While the word was in the king's mouth, a voice came from heaven, saying, 'King Nebuchadnezzar, to you it is declared: sovereignty has been removed from you, and you will be driven away from mankind, and your dwelling place will be with the beasts of the field. You will be given grass to eat like cattle, and seven periods of time will pass over you until you recognize that the Most High is ruler over the realm of mankind and bestows it on whomever He wishes.'" (Daniel 4:31–32)

Because Nebuchadnezzar failed to recognize that God had given him his position, he was forced to graze with cows for seven years. That's one way to fix the pride problem.

Diotrephes was another man with the same attitude (3 John 1:9). He is described as someone who loved "to be first," meaning that he promoted himself to prominence. The late A. T. Robertson once wrote an article about Diotrephes for a religious publication. He renamed him, updated his story using present-day terms, and labeled him the "church boss." Dr. Robertson reported later that twenty deacons had canceled their subscriptions because they thought the article was a personal attack on them.

When we humble ourselves, we understand that God determines who gets promoted on earth and who doesn't.

For not from the east, nor from the west,
    Nor from the desert comes exaltation;
But God is the Judge;
    He puts down one and exalts another. (Psalm 75:6–7)

That means we shouldn't be envious of those who have received a promotion, or be the least bit upset if we've been passed over for one. Advancing to a higher position is ultimately in God's hands.

The late Alex Haley, who wrote *Roots,* had on his office wall a unique picture of a turtle sitting atop a fence post. When people asked him about it, Haley would say, "If you see a turtle on a fence post, you know that he had some help. Any time I start thinking, 'Wow, isn't this marvelous what I've done?' I look at that picture and remember how this turtle, me, got up on that post."[1]

A turtle can't get on top of a fence post unless a hand picks it up and puts it there. Nor can we receive promotion without the hand of God. He puts us where He chooses, whether in a higher or lower position.

Question #4: Do you have trouble submitting to authority?
❑ *Yes* ❑ *No*

Peter wrote: "Submit yourselves for the Lord's sake to every human institution.... Servants, be submissive to your masters with all respect, not only to those who are good and gentle, but also to those who are unreasonable" (1 Peter 2:13, 18).

Sometimes it's easy to submit to the Lord—we just have a hard time submitting to all those human institutions He has established. But if we submit to those in authority only when we agree with them, we become our own authorities. It's a loophole for rebellion. Anyone can submit where there's agreement; it's when those masters are unreasonable that we have the problem.

We are not obligated to submit in cases in which an authority wants us to disobey a higher authority—God's Word. When the high priest told Peter and the apostles to stop teaching about Jesus, they responded, "We must obey God rather than men" (Acts 5:29). Instead of rebelling, they chose to submit to the higher authority.

However, there are many instances when we disagree with the higher authorities simply because we don't like what they want us to do. Although you may not agree with your boss, God wants you to submit to that authority. "Whatever you do, do your work heartily, as for the Lord rather than for men.... It is the Lord Christ whom you serve" (Colossians 3:23, 24).

It is possible to obey our masters without submitting. Obedience is an outward action, while submission is an inward attitude. God calls us not just to obey, but also to submit.

A mother ordered her disobedient son to sit in a corner. After a couple of minutes of sitting, he told his mother, "I'm sitting down on the outside, but I'm standing up on the inside!" He obeyed, but he didn't submit.

A heart that is submissive to God is willing to obey human authorities even when they make unwise decisions. The only way we can submit to unreasonable authorities is through a humble heart that seeks to please the Lord.

Question #5: Are you unwilling to do humiliating jobs?
❑ Yes   ❑ No

In the Greco-Roman world, pride was an attribute to be admired, while humility was something to be shunned at all costs. Jesus taught His disciples the inverse of Greek philosophy. He said, "Whoever wishes to become great among you shall be your servant; and whoever wishes to be first among you shall be slave of all" (Mark 10:43–44). When Jesus said this, everyone thought that He had lost His mind. No one had ever taught them that humility was a virtue and pride was a sin.

Jesus' statement was disappointing news to most folks back then. It isn't very exciting to most people today, either. Not long ago, a television actress said in an interview, "I don't think pride is a sin. I think some idiot made that up."

In our high-tech society where status is in, servants and slaves are definitely out. In order to humble ourselves, we must follow Jesus and not the world. Paul Moody said, "Greatness is not measured by how many people are your servants, but by how many people you serve."

Pride says to itself, "My will be done." Humility says to God, "Thy will be done." It is willing to do any job God asks no matter how insignificant or undignified it might be. If you are too big to do little things, you are too little to do big things. Like ruling nations in eternity, perhaps?

Being a servant doesn't necessarily mean having a low position; it means having a lowly heart. My wife and I went to a restaurant where the meanest waitress we had ever met was "serving" us. She waited on us with the attitude, "My name is Grumpy, and I will be your waitress today. If you need something, you are just going to have to wait your turn. So don't push me!" She was in a servant's position, but she didn't have a servant's heart.

On the other hand, a person can be in a high position and maintain a servant's heart. Many years ago a rider on horseback came across a squad of soldiers who were trying to move a heavy piece of timber. A corporal, one rank above private, was standing by ordering the privates to heave, but the piece of timber was too heavy for them.

The man on the horse asked the corporal, "Why don't you help them?"

The soldier replied, "Me? Because I'm a corporal, that's why."

The stranger dismounted and took his place with the privates. Then he said, "Now, all together—heave." The big piece of timber moved into place. Then the stranger mounted his horse and addressed the corporal. "The next time you have a piece of timber for your men to handle, corporal, send for the commander-in-chief." The horseman was George Washington.[2]

Question #6: Do you look down on anyone?
❏ *Yes* ❏ *No*

Archie Bunker once said, "I'm not prejudiced. I love all those inferior people." If we are humble, we will never look down on anyone. We can only look up to them. God instructs us to regard others as more important than ourselves (Philippians 2:3).

Our viewpoint always determines our opinions of others. Pride sets itself up in a higher position so it can look down on people. Former heavyweight boxing champion Muhammad Ali boasted, "I am the greatest." The apostle Paul boasted, "I am the least" (Ephesians 3:8, NLT). Ali thought that he was more important than everyone else, while Paul viewed everyone else as more important than himself.

We can look down on others without realizing it. During Sunday school, a teacher told the children in her class about the Pharisee and the tax-gatherer praying in the temple (Luke 18:10–14). She said that the Pharisee prayed, "God, I thank You that I'm not like other people," while the tax-gatherer said, "God, be merciful to me, a sinner." The teacher explained how the pious, self-righteous attitude of the Pharisee caused him to look down on the tax-gatherer. At the end of the class, she asked one little boy to close in prayer. He prayed, "God, I thank You that I'm not like that Pharisee."

The Bible doesn't teach that others are more important than we are, but that we are to *regard* others as more important (Philippians 2:3). Humility doesn't mean that we put ourselves down, but that we lift others up. Although all people are of equal value in God's eyes, from our viewpoint others should appear more significant.

Question #7: Do you brag about your strengths instead of your weaknesses? ❏ *Yes* ❏ *No*

Admitting our weaknesses opens the way to receiving the power of God. Pride likes to boast in its strength, while humility boasts in its weakness. Paul said, "Most gladly, therefore, I will rather boast about my weaknesses, so that the power of Christ may dwell in me" (2 Corinthians 12:9).

Although it is tempting to brag about our achievements, it's better to keep silent and let the accomplishments speak for themselves. A chicken lays one egg and cackles

A chicken lays one egg and cackles about it, while a salmon lays ten thousand eggs and doesn't say a word.

about it, while a salmon lays ten thousand eggs and doesn't say a word.

Our educational credentials can also be a source of pride. Someone once said that a diploma is like the curl on the tail of a pig. It doesn't mean very much, but it sure does tickle the ham to which it is attached. Paul said that he counted his great heritage and education as rubbish compared to the value of gaining Christ (Philippians 3:8). Humility acknowledges that we are weak, but He is strong.

GRADING YOUR TEST

Well, how did you do on the Humility Test? If you answered *yes* to any of the above questions, you have areas of pride in your life. The solution to the pride problem is to take some steps downward:

> Clothe yourselves with humility toward one another, for GOD IS OPPOSED TO THE PROUD, BUT GIVES GRACE TO THE HUMBLE. Therefore humble yourselves under the mighty hand of God, that He may exalt you at the proper time. (1 Peter 5:5–6)

Other than God, the only one who can "humble yourself" is you. When we humble ourselves under God's mighty hand, we submit ourselves to His control so that He can guide us in any way He wishes. When we are humble, we recognize how little we are compared to almighty God and that He deserves all praise and glory.

A rooster named Chanticleer was a vain bird that prided himself on his accomplishments. He was proudest of the fact that his crowing caused the sun to rise each morning. Every morning he crowed. Every morning the sun rose.

One morning Chanticleer overslept. When he awoke, he was surprised to see that the sun was already up and that it had happened without any help from him. He then realized that he could not take credit for the rising of the sun each day. However, there was something he could do. Chanticleer declared, "If by my crowing I cannot bring in the dawn, then by my crowing I can celebrate its coming."[3]

What accomplishments have you been crowing about? Although you can't take credit for the things God does, you can certainly glorify Him.

That's humility. Shining the spotlight on God, not ourselves.

MAKING THE MOST OF YOUR OPPORTUNITY

- Admit a weakness or a failure to someone you trust.
- Apologize to someone you might have hurt.
- Make a sincere attempt to reconcile with an enemy.
- Cheerfully obey an unreasonable employer or authority in your life.

chapter eleven

GOD'S UPSIDE-DOWN KINGDOM

"Whoever wishes to be first among you shall be slave of all."

MARK 10:44

Have you ever "claimed" a verse from the Bible? Sometimes we like to select certain promises from God's Word that we can apply to our lives. And that's good. But I've noticed a lot of passages in the Bible that get overlooked. Often these verses are in the same chapter as our favorite promises, but for some reason we don't see them. These Scriptures command us to be content in all circumstances, love our enemies, put away bitterness, and give up our possessions. Yet hardly anyone wants to claim these verses.

God's Word is not a cafeteria where we can pass over the asparagus to get to the dessert. We can't pick and choose our favorite passages and ignore the rest. Here are some commonly claimed verses and their usually unclaimed siblings:

VERSES WE LIKE TO CLAIM	VERSES WE DON'T LIKE TO CLAIM
My God will supply all your needs according to His riches in glory in Christ Jesus. (Philippians 4:19)	I have learned to be content in whatever circumstances I am. (Philippians 4:11)
"Give, and it will be given to you. They will pour into your lap a good measure— pressed down, shaken together, and running over." (Luke 6:38)	"Love your enemies, do good to those who hate you, bless those who curse you, pray for those who mistreat you." (Luke 6:27–28)
In Him we have redemption through His blood, the forgiveness of our trespasses, according to the riches of His grace. (Ephesians 1:7)	Let all bitterness and wrath and anger and clamor and slander be put away from you, along with all malice. Be kind to one another, tender-hearted, forgiving each other, just as Christ also has forgiven you. (Ephesians 4:31–32)
"Blessed are those who mourn, for they shall be comforted." (Matthew 5:4)	"Blessed are you when people insult you and persecute you, and falsely say all kinds of evil against you because of Me." (Matthew 5:11)
Beloved, I pray that in all respects you may prosper and be in good health, just as your soul prospers. (3 John 1:2)	"So then, none of you can be My disciple who does not give up all his own possessions." (Luke 14:33)

Just when I think I have my theology figured out, God starts throwing curveballs: "Do good to those who hate you." "Bless those who curse you." "You are blessed when people speak evil against you falsely."

And here's the clincher. "Those who want to be first must become slaves."

To the natural mind, God's kingdom is upside-down. How do we get to the top by going to the bottom? How can ruling come from serving, or glory from suffering? That's what James and John couldn't figure out.

CLAIMING THRONES

James and John wanted to claim a promise from God. They told Jesus, "We want You to do for us whatever we ask of You" (Mark 10:35).

Most of us pray that way, don't we? We like to tell Jesus what to do. Ask not what you can do for your God, but what your God can do for you.

Rather than rebuking His disciples for their presumption, Jesus asked, "What do you want Me to do for you?" (v. 36). (There is a huge theological difference, by the way, between us telling Jesus what to do and Jesus asking us what we want Him to do.)

James and John could have asked for wisdom like Solomon did when God asked him that same question (1 Kings 3:5, 9). Instead, they asked for chairs: "Grant that we may sit, one on Your right and one on Your left, in Your glory" (Mark 10:37).

It seems to me that James and John thought that not everyone received the same eternal reward; otherwise, they would not have requested the highest thrones in the kingdom of God. Jesus had been teaching them that another world existed beyond their present life and that some positions in God's kingdom were better than others. In fact, Jesus had guaranteed the disciples twelve thrones in His coming kingdom as part of their reward for following Him (Matthew 19:28). What they didn't understand was that in God's upside-down kingdom, to get higher they had to go lower.

James and John said, "It's nice to make the top twelve, Jesus, but we have higher aspirations than those ten other guys. We would like to reserve a couple of the executive suites. Nonsmoking, please."

Jesus answered, "You do not know what you are asking for."

God usually answers prayer in one of four ways: yes, no, wait, or you do not know what you are asking for. The answer to their request was behind door number four.

It was true: James and John did not know what they were asking for. Most of us don't know what we are asking for when we pray, either. We don't always understand the ramifications of our requests. Jesus cautioned them that such elite positions come at a costly price. Instead of a throne, He offered them a cup. "Are you able to drink the cup that I drink?" (Mark 10:38).

By dying on the cross, Jesus did indeed drink the cup. He was crucified with a thief on His right and another thief on His left. James and John didn't ask to be on those crosses, but to wear the crowns on His right and left. They wanted recognition, not crucifixion.

And isn't that just like us? We're anxious to claim the throne of glory, but not the cup of suffering. After some deliberation, I'm sure, James and John said that they would indeed be willing to drink the cup in exchange for the top positions (v. 39).

Of course, the other disciples weren't too happy about their little scheme. They had also been saying, "Mirror, mirror on the wall, who's the greatest of us all?" (Mark 9:33–34, 10:41). It offended them that James and John asked for the top spots. In the back of their minds, perhaps they too had been dreaming of ruling in the highest positions. Maybe they had been planning to pull Jesus aside and make the same request.

So Jesus called the disciples together and said, "Look, guys, you are thinking all wrong. My kingdom doesn't work like the empires of this world. In My kingdom, everything is upside-down. Instead of working your way up the ladder, work your way *down* it. The way to the throne is through the cup. To become a king, you must first become a slave. When everyone else is grabbing for power and positions, you grab for the scrub brush and toilet cleaner. If you want the highest position, volunteer for the lowest position, and then you will be the greatest in My kingdom."

Although James and John loved Jesus and were devoted to following Him, they were confused concerning the character of God's kingdom. Many of us have the same misunderstanding, despite our true love for Christ. We can utilize the wrong spirit, standard, and strategy in our quest for greatness.

THE WRONG SPIRIT

Jesus told James and John that they didn't know what they were asking for. On another occasion, He told them that they didn't know what kind of spirit they had. When the Samaritans didn't welcome the disciples, the dynamic duo almost called down fire from heaven to consume the people in the village (Luke 9:52–54). Jesus rebuked them, saying, "You do not know what kind of spirit you are of" (v. 55). They were blind to the fact that they had a wrong spirit operating in them.

Jesus nicknamed these two firecrackers the "Sons of Thunder" (Mark 3:17). That title sounds like it belongs to a couple of thugs from a motorcycle gang, not a pair of mild-mannered net menders, doesn't it?

Some Bible scholars believe that James and John were called the Sons of Thunder because of their zeal and passion. The problem with fiery zeal is that those who have it tend to get burned by their mistakes. Although zealous people are quick to take charge, they are prone to act impulsively and make wrong decisions, which they later regret. Faith and zeal without love and humility will destroy everyone in its path.

Think about it. Were these guys qualified to be *numeros uno* and *dos,* the top rulers in Jesus' kingdom? Wouldn't you be a little nervous if James and John were sitting on the highest thrones monitoring your life? It can be dangerous if the person holding that scepter has the wrong spirit. If you mess up one time, he is likely to call fire down from heaven and turn you into a Crispy Critter. James and John were ready to ignite a whole village like charcoal because it didn't roll out the welcome mat for them.

Full of zeal? Absolutely.

Full of compassion? Hardly.

This is why Jesus told them, "You don't know what kind of spirit is motivating you. You're not ready to sit on thrones, instructing people what to do. You need a change of heart before you can be in charge of others. I'm building a kingdom of servants. Those who have servant spirits will receive the highest positions in My kingdom."

How do you react when you are mistreated? Are you ready to call down fire from heaven? If so, you may be operating out of the wrong spirit.

THE WRONG STANDARD

The disciples had been discussing which one of them was the greatest (Mark 9:34). They based their standard of greatness on how they compared with others. They used the wrong measuring stick. Instead of humbling themselves before one another, they compared themselves with each other. That's why the other disciples became indignant when they heard James and John's request.

Paul reminded us that we should not think more highly of ourselves than we ought (Romans 12:3). If we compare ourselves with others, we will become either proud or discouraged—and neither is from God. We will put others down, or we will put ourselves down. Comparing ourselves with others produces a distorted perspective of both ourselves and others.

Are you comparing yourself in order to determine your greatness?

THE WRONG STRATEGY

Everybody is consumed with being number one. College football fans look into the camera and say, "We're number one!" It's the same at the NBA Championship, the Super Bowl, the World Series, or the Stanley Cup.

The problem is that no matter in which sport you're number one, your reign lasts only until the next season begins. Blink, and it's over. A different team often captures the title a few months later. In this world you won't stay number one for very long. Someone is always waiting to unseat you.

The disciples also got caught up in the "we-are-number-one" mentality. They were trying to achieve prominence by ruling over others instead of serving under others. Like them, we tend to think that we acquire significance by reaching the highest levels of success.

We have let the world define greatness for us. Our society has built itself on the philosophy of the devil instead of on the wisdom of God. As long as we believe Satan's big lie that our lives are insignificant unless we are on top, we will live in a constant state of dejection, worthlessness, and strife.

To overcome this incorrect way of thinking, we need to modify our strategy. We must change audiences. Which audience are we trying to please: people in this world, or God in heaven? Instead of trying to become great by doing what this world dictates, we must use God's dictionary to find out what greatness really is.

God isn't interested in us being famous in the world's eyes, but in us being faithful in His eyes. We should live to please the unseen audience. Once we view life from heaven's point of view, every person becomes significant and every job becomes important. We will find meaning in everything, even in the smallest responsibilities. We won't view changing diapers, washing dishes, and visiting the retirement home as mundane chores, but as crucial assignments for the kingdom of God. In God's dictionary, greatness is not found on the title page, but in the footnotes.

It doesn't make sense, does it? In God's upside-down kingdom, the way up is down. The way to be first is to be last. To be great we must be least, and to rule we must serve. People want to have good service, but they don't want to be good servants. If we want to be great, we need to be good servants. And if we want to be first forever, we must first become slaves.

God isn't interested in us being famous in the world's eyes, but in us being faithful in His eyes.

What is the difference between a servant and a slave? In New Testament times, a servant was hired by his master, as in the story of the prodigal son (Luke 15:11–23). A slave, on the other hand, was owned by his master. He had no rights whatsoever. Jesus taught that if you want to be first in eternity, you must give up your rights and spend the rest of your life giving yourself away. Most people don't want to hear that. That's why there are so few applicants for the position.

If Jesus had told us how to be great in this world—how to become president, a famous actor, a successful athlete, or a prominent businessman—everyone would be scrambling to follow His instructions. People are always anxious to make it big in this world. But when Jesus tells us how to be great *forever,* we want to bypass the process. We aren't willing to drink the cup—unless it contains our favorite beverage.

Do we really believe what Jesus said about greatness in eternity? If so, we must turn the other cheek when persecuted, forgive those who have hurt us, love our enemies, and find every way possible to joyfully serve Him.

GODLY SLAVES FINISH FIRST

Nice guys may finish last, but godly slaves will finish first. God has saved us for all eternity, but He also gives us an amazing opportunity to attain greater positions in His kingdom. Those who serve humbly during their earthly lives will be exalted in eternity. Here are four characteristics of a godly slave.

1) A godly slave isn't picky about his jobs.

E. Stanley Jones once told a story about a man in India who became a Christian. The man was a Brahmin convert, meaning that he was from the upper caste in India. Everyone in the community was expected to participate in the chores, including the cleaning of latrines. Stanley Jones told him that there are no unacceptable jobs for the child of God and that when a person is converted to the lordship of Jesus, he should have no problem cleaning latrines. The Indian man replied, "Brother Stanley, I'm converted, but not that far."

Many of us are converted, but not that far. Godly slaves aren't choosy about their jobs. They simply obey whatever the Master tells them to do. Godly slaves don't say:

- "I'm not going to do that."
- "I don't do windows."
- "No one's going to tell *me* what to do!"
- "I don't have to put up with this."
- "They don't realize who I am."
- "They don't appreciate all I do around here!"
- "I don't get any respect."

When I first enrolled in seminary, I made an appointment to talk to the dean of men to see if I could get a room in the dormitory. When I walked into his office, the first thing he asked was, "Are you applying for the janitor's job?"

"No," I said. "I'm here to see if any rooms are available in the dorm."

"I'm sorry; the dormitory is full. We'll put you on the waiting list. But if you know anyone who wants a job as janitor, please send him to see me."

I told him that I wasn't interested and thanked him for his time. When I left his office and walked outside, I prayed, *Lord, please provide a room for me.* God stopped me on the sidewalk and spoke to my heart, "Go take the job."

Take the job? I prayed for a room, not a job. But I knew in my heart I needed to obey. Immediately I did an about-face, walked into the dean's office, and said, "I'll take that janitor's job." He hired me on the spot.

At first, I had to battle my pride. I thought about how over-qualified I was—I had a college degree and was working on my Master's. I was given a janitor's shirt and a little pushcart stocked with soap, gloves, toilet paper, toilet bowl cleaner, and a brush. Every day I pushed that cart down the hallway, cleaned toilets, scrubbed showers, and emptied trashcans.

It wasn't long before I discovered that cleaning those bathrooms in the men's dorm was part of my spiritual education. I learned to do the jobs that no one else wanted. As I cleaned those toilets every day, I made a surprising discovery. God spoke to my heart more clearly than I had ever heard Him before. I meditated on Scriptures as I worked, and God gave me insights into His Word. I then realized that cleaning toilets was part of my training for ministry. If I wasn't willing to serve God as a custodian, how could He trust me with other responsibilities?

I spent my entire three years in seminary cleaning toilets and attending classes. I'm convinced that half of what I learned in seminary was in the classrooms and the other half was in the bathrooms. I also learned to respect and thank janitors for the work they do. God used that job to teach me that in whatever tasks He calls me to do in life, I am actually serving Him.

Godly slaves don't care about receiving recognition, but only in pleasing their Master. They have no qualms about any job that they are asked to do.

Are there any jobs you refuse to do?

2) A godly slave always does his best for his master.
In the parable of the talents, a slave's master was gone for a long time on a journey. When the master returned, he examined his

slave's work and said, "Well done, good and faithful slave" (Matthew 25:21). The slave did his best work even though his master wasn't there to observe him.

A godly slave can be counted on to do his or her best, even when no one but God is watching. When Michelangelo was painting the Sistine Chapel in Rome, he was seen meticulously painting in a secluded area that was out of view. Someone asked him why he spent so much time painting in an area where no one would see it. Michelangelo replied, "Because I will see it."

We need to perform our best work for the Lord, even if no human sees it. Remember Truman Burbank's unseen audience? Most of us don't need to look for more things to do for God. We just need to do a better job with what God has already assigned us to do.

Former Secretary of State Henry Kissinger once asked his assistant to prepare a report for him. The assistant worked on it day and night. Finally he completed the task and gave it to his boss. An hour later, Kissinger sent it back with a note attached saying, "Do it again."

The assistant stayed up all night redoing the report and in the morning turned it in to Kissinger. One hour later, Kissinger again returned the report, and again his note read, "Do it again."

After rewriting the report a third time, the assistant delivered it to Kissinger personally and said, "Sir, I've done the very best I can do."

Kissinger replied, "In that case, I'll read it now."

3) A godly slave serves joyfully.
A godly slave always serves cheerfully. Psalm 100:2 says, "Serve the LORD with gladness." Maybe you are serving the Lord—but are you doing it cheerfully?

A shut-in elderly Christian lady once said, "I have two daughters who take turns cleaning my house. When one of my daughters cleans my house, she does a good job but leaves the impression that I'm a terrible burden to her. But when my other daughter cleans my house, she is so joyful. She makes me feel that she loves me. When she cleans, she doesn't just pick up the place; she picks up my spirit, too."

Although both daughters were Christians, one served out of obligation and the other out of jubilation. Their opposing attitudes in serving influenced the way their mother felt.

Is it possible that our attitudes in serving the Lord influence how we make Him feel? Does it bother God when we don't serve Him joyfully? Moses told Israel, "Because you did not serve the LORD your God with joy and a glad heart, for the abundance of all things; therefore you shall serve your enemies whom the LORD shall send against you" (Deuteronomy 28:47–48). Our attitude does make a difference.

4) A godly slave serves everyone.

Notice two very important words in the following verse. "And whoever wishes to be first among you shall be slave *of all*" (Mark 10:44). It's not hard to be a slave of someone we respect. Sometimes it's even fun to be a servant to a hero or celebrity. But what about serving the rest of the bunch—the nitwits, misfits, and nincompoops out there? What about those who don't appreciate what we do? And how about that intolerable boss? Serve him too?

When Jesus told us to be a slave of all, He meant all of the above. A godly slave is not selective about whom he or she will serve.

OVER ONE BILLION SERVED

I believe that we would be shocked if we knew who will get the highest positions in the kingdom of heaven. It'll probably be people that we've never heard of. I suspect that some of them will have been literal slaves during their earthly lives. I also wouldn't be surprised to see some faithful hamburger flippers in heavenly high places. That would be like God—to promote those who were overlooked here on earth.

Remember, in God's kingdom, everything is upside-down. The greatest in the next life is the slave in this life. The ones now on the bottom will end up on top. So start working your way *down* the ladder. One day, perhaps a couple of million years from now, you will be glad you did.

MAKING THE MOST OF YOUR OPPORTUNITY

- Wash the dishes after dinner for your wife (or take the trash out for your husband).
- Find a job that no one wants, and cheerfully do it.
- Go out of your way to help a neighbor.
- Volunteer in the church nursery.

chapter twelve

LITTLE THINGS ARE BIG THINGS

"He who is faithful in a very little thing is faithful also in much."

LUKE 16:10

Martha Berry lived from 1866 to 1942. She founded the Berry School for needy children at Mount Berry, Georgia. On one occasion she asked Henry Ford for one million dollars to assist her school. He didn't donate the huge amount that she requested. Instead, he gave her a dime.

Although she could have become bitter at his insulting gesture, she graciously accepted the dime and bought some peanuts for her schoolboys to plant. The next season they harvested the peanuts and used the entire crop to plant a larger field. Eventually they harvested and sold enough peanuts to buy a piano for their music students.

Martha wrote a letter to Mr. Ford telling him how they had used his dime to harvest enough peanuts to buy a piano for their school. Ford was so impressed by her faithfulness that he invited her to Detroit and personally handed her one million dollars.[1] Because she had proved herself faithful with a dime, Henry Ford knew that she would be faithful with a million.

Most of us would love to manage a million dollars. But we never think about being faithful with our dimes. Ironically, it's how we handle the little things on earth that will determine what we manage in eternity. This means that little things are actually big things. Jesus said, "He who is faithful in a very little thing is faithful also in much; and he who is unrighteous in a very little thing is unrighteous also in much" (Luke 16:10).

Why would God give dynamite to someone who can't handle a firecracker?

How we manage little things indicates what we would do if we had more. Why would God give dynamite to someone who can't handle a firecracker? It would be foolish to give greater responsibilities to someone who had proven unfaithful with smaller jobs.

As we have seen in the previous chapters, humility reveals our attitudes, and serving puts them into action. But faithfulness *proves* that our attitudes and actions are genuine. Anyone can humbly serve—for a while. But will it stick? Is it real, or just a flash in the pan? All that glitters is not God. Faithfulness will pass the tests of responsibility, loyalty, and time. Eternal responsibilities will be assigned according to faithfulness with our Opportunity.

LITTLE HOUSE ON THE PRAIRIE

A friend of mine here in Kansas once told me that his wife wanted to move to a larger house. She had a problem keeping their smaller house clean but promised him that if they bought a larger house she would keep it spotless. He lovingly told her, "Honey, if you can't keep a little house clean, how do you expect to keep a big house clean?"

Our earthly duties are the "little house" to prepare us for eternity. The slaves who were faithful with a few things were put in charge of many things. Only when we have been faithful in administering the smallest details can we be trusted to handle bigger things. But if we aren't faithful with our earthly responsibilities, why would God want to entrust His eternal treasure to us? Jesus said, "Therefore if you have not been faithful in the use of unrighteous wealth, who will entrust the true riches to you?" (Luke 16:11).

We must not forget that this life is simply a temporary world to prepare us for God's eternal kingdom. Everything that will happen in the next world will be based on our faithfulness right now.

Unfortunately, a couple of myths paralyze people and keep them from taking action.

MYTH #1: HAVING MORE MONEY WILL MAKE ME MORE FAITHFUL

Some people say, "If I only had a million dollars, my faithfulness would increase. I don't make enough money to be faithful with it."

Jesus never said that our faithfulness would increase if we were given more. Faithfulness is always found in the present, not in the future. He said, "He who is *faithful* in a very little thing is *faithful* also in much." An increase in our assets will not increase our faithfulness.

A missionary once asked a new convert, "Pablo, if you had a hundred sheep, would you give fifty of them to the Lord's work?"

He answered, "You know I would gladly give them."

"Pablo, if you had fifty cows, would you give twenty-five to the Lord's work?"

"Yes, you know I would be more than happy do that."

Again the missionary asked, "Pablo, if you had two pigs, would you give one of them to the Lord's work?"

"That's not fair," Pablo replied. "You know I have two pigs."

Many people are extremely generous in theory but not in practice. They say, "If only I had a million dollars, I would give half of it away." That is simply not true. If we aren't faithfully giving even ten percent of our money right now, we wouldn't give away half a million dollars if we had it.

It's easy to sacrifice in theory. But the truth is that we wouldn't be any more faithful in our giving and stewardship if we had a million dollars than we are right now. God holds us accountable "according to what a person has, *not according to what he does not have*" (2 Corinthians 8:12).

Would four and a half million dollars be enough money to make you more faithful? In 1992 a well-known professional baseball player who had a salary of three million dollars and a signing bonus of one and a half million dollars was forced to file for bankruptcy. His expensive hobbies and high standard of living had left him one million dollars in debt. Having a fortune didn't make him a faithful money manager.

Oseola McCarty, on the other hand, washed clothes for a living for seventy years of her life. On September 26, 1999, she died at age ninety-one. Miss McCarty earned fifty cents per load doing laundry for affluent families in Hattiesburg, Mississippi. She deposited a little bit in a bank account each week, and by the time she retired she had accumulated $250,000. "It was more than I could use," she said. Rather than spending the money on herself, she gave $150,000 to the University of Southern Mississippi to help African-American young people attend college.

The baseball player couldn't live on four and a half million dollars, but a few pennies consistently saved over a lifetime became a fortune for Oseola McCarty. A little bit of faithfulness over a lifetime produces the accumulated effect of great abundance. Their vast differences in income didn't make any difference in the way they managed their money. Having more money didn't make the baseball player more faithful, and having less money didn't cause Oseola McCarty to be less faithful.

God wants us to be faithful *where we are* right now, with *what we have* right now. Faithfulness begins in the present and extends over a long period of time. If God chooses to increase our income, then our faithfulness will already be established. If we aren't faithful with what we have now, however, we won't be faithful with what we receive in the future.

Howard Hendricks said, "It's not what you would do with a million dollars, if a million were your lot. It's what you are doing right now, with the buck and a quarter you've got."

MYTH #2: A BETTER SET OF CIRCUMSTANCES WILL MAKE ME MORE FAITHFUL

Many people think that a change in circumstances would make them more faithful. They assume that if they had a promotion or a better job, they would work more diligently. But getting promoted won't make you any more faithful than you are right now. Ironically, that may be why you haven't received the better position you've been hoping for. Why would your boss want to give you a promotion if you haven't been dependable so far?

Do you have to be constantly reminded to get your work done? Do you have a problem with being late or with putting off work that needs to be finished? Are you currently doing your best work? Do you complain about your present job? If this is what you are like now, if you did receive a promotion, you would still complain, procrastinate, and be irresponsible—even with your new set of circumstances. The problem is not with your job, but with your heart.

I know a man who always complained about his job and employers. He was undependable and didn't make the best use of his time at work. A different company was looking for a manager to complete a large project in this man's area of expertise. He applied for the position and was hired. He gladly made the occupational change and started out very industrious and enthusiastic.

It didn't take long, though, until he began complaining and displaying the same inefficiency he had shown in his previous job. The company took notice of his slothfulness and poor attitude and decided to let him go. Moving to a better job hadn't improved his attitude, faithfulness, or dependability. He was unrighteous in little, and he was also unrighteous in much—just like Jesus said.

WHAT DOES "FAITHFULNESS" MEAN?

Our faithfulness on earth will affect our positions for all eternity. Since it's that important, let's take a look at what it entails. Faithfulness covers four areas: excellence, integrity, dependability, and perseverance.

Faithfulness Means Excellence

Faithfulness doesn't necessarily mean doing *more,* but doing things *better.* Doing our best in every situation is one proof of faithfulness. It includes our financial stewardship, family responsibilities, job assignments, and ministry opportunities. God is primarily concerned with how we handle the unnoticed, everyday deeds that don't make the newspaper headlines on earth. In God's eyes, little things truly are big.

Faithfulness Means Integrity

A storeowner interviewed a young man for a job. He asked, "If I hire you to work in my store, will you be honest and truthful?" The young man answered, "I will be honest and truthful whether you hire me or not."

Faithfulness means that we are above moral reproach at all times. Remember: God still sees us, even when no one is watching.

Faithfulness Means Dependability

A lazy worker retired, and a dinner was given in his honor to present him an award. The toastmaster said, "As a token of our appreciation, we would like to give you this watch to serve as a constant reminder of your faithfulness to our company. It has to be wound frequently, it's always a little late, and it quits working every day at a quarter till four."

Does that describe you? Faithful people can be relied upon to fulfill their commitments. When a job is delegated to a faithful worker, the boss never has to worry if the job will get done.

Faithfulness Means Perseverance

Vance Havner once said, "Too many people go up like rockets and come down like rocks." Lots of people start running the race of life with a flash, but few finish well. Others might get sidetracked or drop out of the race, but we must keep running with our eyes fixed on Jesus. Faithfulness means that we persevere to the finish line.

Some people drop out of the race because they get offended. A few get bummed out; others get burned out, or so they claim. But to Satan's delight, all the dropouts are sitting useless on the shelf. They no longer use their God-given abilities to fulfill their God-given callings. They have buried their talents and forfeited eternal rewards that could have been theirs. "Be faithful until death, and I will give you the crown of life" (Revelation 2:10).

No More Excuses

Have you been making excuses for your lack of faithfulness? Think you need more money? Try being faithful with what little money you have now. Do you feel that your boss is unfair? Begin serving God through your employment, and those "injustices" will cease to trouble you. Bothered because others aren't doing their share of work? Forget what they do, and concentrate on what you can do. You will not be judged by what others do, but according to your own attitude and faithfulness.

Don't put it off any longer. Today, this very moment, is the time to begin your journey of faithfulness. Start planting your peanuts—those little things. One day you may be surprised at the harvest you reap.

Making the Most of Your Opportunity

- Increase your giving to the Lord on a regular basis.
- Finish all those jobs you started.
- Improve the quality of your work to the best of your ability.
- Don't make commitments you can't keep.

chapter thirteen

IT'S A
WONDERFUL LIFE

No eye has seen, no ear has heard, no mind has conceived
what God has prepared for those who love him.

1 CORINTHIANS 2:9, NIV

I n the movie *It's a Wonderful Life*, George Bailey's life from
childhood to adulthood was being watched from heaven.
When George was a boy, he saved his brother Harry from
drowning. Harry later became a war hero. After George grew up, he
encountered a series of misfortunes in his business and personal
life. Thinking that he had no reason to live, he decided to end his
life by jumping off a bridge.

An angel named Clarence, dressed inconspicuously as an
elderly gentleman, stopped him from taking his life. The angel tried
to tell him how valuable his life was, but George refused to believe
him. In an effort to convince George of his importance, Clarence
showed him what the world would have been like if he had never

been born. Earth's history was altered to exclude the life of George Bailey.

When George viewed the world with his life omitted, he discovered that lots of things in his town had changed. He went to the cemetery and saw a tombstone, which revealed that his brother had died as a boy. Clarence said, "Your brother Harry Bailey broke through the ice and drowned at the age of nine."

George said, "That's a lie. Harry Bailey went to war and won the Congressional Medal of Honor. He saved the lives of every man on that transport."

Clarence answered, "Every man on that transport died. Harry wasn't there to save them because you weren't there to save Harry. You see, George, you really had a wonderful life. Don't you see what a mistake it would be to throw it away?"

When George finally realized the significance of his existence, God allowed him to return to his earthly life. Although his problems remained the same, his perspective had changed. The circumstances that had previously depressed him now didn't bother him at all. George decided to view his earthly existence as a privilege instead of a problem, and he discovered that life was truly wonderful.

You, too, have a wonderful life. You have been given a chance to start life over again with a new perspective. And you now see, as George Bailey discovered, that God has placed you on this planet for a reason. He is giving you the opportunity to participate in His plan for the ages.

Seeing the big picture will help you understand how the little pieces of the puzzle fit into God's plan. The problems that you face every day are merely tests to prepare you for your eternal destiny. Viewed in that way, life takes on a whole new meaning.

What then, should you do with the rest of your life? Restructuring your priorities is a good place to start.

SETTING NEW PRIORITIES

To have a wonderful life, we need to reset our priorities. The first item on our new agenda is to seek the kingdom of God and His righteousness above all else (Matthew 6:33). If we get the top button of a shirt buttoned wrong, all of the other buttons will also be off. Many people have everything in their lives out of order because they haven't fastened the kingdom of God button first.

Here are some ideas for how to button down your priorities. Remember, this life is your only chance to affect your eternity.

Love God
Someone once asked Jesus, "What is the great commandment in the Law?" To put it another way, "Lord, what's the top button in life?"
Jesus answered him:

> "'YOU SHALL LOVE THE LORD YOUR GOD WITH ALL YOUR
> HEART, AND WITH ALL YOUR SOUL, AND WITH ALL YOUR
> MIND.' This is the great and foremost commandment. The
> second is like it, 'YOU SHALL LOVE YOUR NEIGHBOR AS
> YOURSELF.'" (Matthew 22:37–39)

The top button is to love God. The second button is to love people. It's that simple. Do that and every other button in life will fall into place. When we love God and others, we will automatically fulfill everything He wants us to do. But the moment we stop loving God, we start loving ourselves. And then we get all the buttons messed up.

There was once a married couple who didn't love each other. The day they got married, the husband handed his wife a list of chores for her to follow. He insisted that she do all the tasks on her list every day. The wife worked hard to accomplish her assigned duties, but she was miserable as she performed them. Ironing his clothes, preparing his meals, cleaning house—every task was burdensome. Although she obeyed all his rules, she never enjoyed a loving relationship with her husband.

Then one day her husband died. After several years had passed, she fell in love with another man and got married. The new husband never required her to do anything, much less a list of jobs. Instead, he showered her with love and did everything he could to make her happy.

One day this wife was joyfully cleaning house when she discovered her first husband's list of commands tucked away in a drawer. As she read the paper, it dawned on her that she was performing every task on the list, but now she was serving with joy instead of misery. Her love for her second husband inspired her to automatically do the same jobs that her first husband had required. She had served her first husband out of duty, but she served her second husband out of love.

God wants us to serve Him out of jubilation, not obligation. Legalism adds weights to our work, but love gives wings to our service. Which describes the way you serve the Lord?

Be Thankful

A little boy was asked to say the prayer at Thanksgiving dinner. After thanking God for the food and his family, he ran out of things to say. Then he prayed, "Now let me tell You some things I'm *not* thankful for."

Most of us separate everything into two categories—the things we are thankful for and the things we aren't thankful for. God says that we need to combine everything into one category and give thanks for all of it. "In everything give thanks; for *this is God's will* for you in Christ Jesus" (1 Thessalonians 5:18).

God's will for us begins with a thankful attitude. If you are searching for the will of God, you will discover it inside your own grateful heart. Happiness comes looking for us when we start giving thanks.

After the Soviet invasion of Afghanistan, actor Kirk Douglas flew to Pakistan to do a documentary. He sat on the ground with the elders of an Afghan tribe, who were eating with their fingers out of a common bowl. He told them, "In my country, today is Thanksgiving Day. Every year we set aside one day to give thanks for all that we have."

The leader of the elders, a man with a long white beard, nodded his head. Through an interpreter he said, "In my country, we give thanks every day."[1]

This just goes to show that thankfulness isn't determined by how much we have, but by what's inside our hearts. Thanksgiving isn't a holiday, but a holy way. We need to be thankful for all things, every day.

The attitude of gratitude is important for several reasons:

- Thankfulness acknowledges that God is our provider.
- Thankfulness prevents a complaining spirit.
- Thankfulness creates a positive outlook on life.
- Thankfulness invites joy to dwell in our hearts.

What you look for in life will determine whether you become grateful or hateful. Before you do anything else, first take a good, long look inside. Make sure your heart is thankful, and then you can do the task at hand.

Enjoy Living

Jesus didn't just come to get us into heaven, but to get heaven into us. He said, "I came that they may have life, and have it abundantly" (John 10:10). What does it mean to have abundant life? It means:

- Jesus came to give us *eternal* life, so that we can live endlessly.
- Jesus came to give *spiritual* life, so that we can live correctly.
- Jesus came to give us *abundant* life, so that we can live joyfully.

God "richly supplies us with all things to enjoy" (1 Timothy 6:17). Why would God give us all things to enjoy if we couldn't enjoy them?

One day I was driving my car on a rural highway in Kansas. I was between destinations, with nothing to do but drive and watch the flat land and telephone poles pass. Then God spoke to my heart: "Enjoy the moment."

Jesus didn't just come to get us into heaven, but to get heaven into us.

Enjoy the moment? What was there to enjoy?

I then realized that joy is a decision I make. I need to take pleasure in every minute of life, not just the exciting times. God wants us to draw joy from every moment, every circumstance. The goal in life is not to rush from one destination to the next. How often we hurry from event to event and fail to enjoy the moments in between. The joy of life is in the journey as much as it is in the destination. The goal in life is not to check everything off our chore list as we hurry through each day.

Recently I planted some bushes. Many people might consider that an insignificant event, but if God took the time to create the bushes, shouldn't I take the time to enjoy them? "Whether, then, you eat or drink or whatever you do, do all to the glory of God" (1 Corinthians 10:31).

What applies to bushes certainly applies to God's most precious creation—people. Enjoy your fellowship with others. Enjoy spending time with your family. Savor the moments. If you don't, the life that God wants you to enjoy will pass you by, just like those telephone poles.

Don't Quit

Colossians 4:17 says, "Take heed to the ministry which you have received in the Lord, that you may fulfill it." If you've dropped out of the race, it's time to get up and start running again. It's not too late. The contest isn't over until you die. Are you reaching all of your God-given potential?

Michelangelo attempted to carve forty-four statues during his life, but he finished only fourteen. Although we are familiar with some of his work, such as the statue of *David*, the thirty that he didn't finish are also intriguing. One is a huge chunk of marble from which he sculpted only an elbow. Another shows a leg, thigh, knee, foot, and toes, but the rest of the body is locked inside the marble.

Many of us are like those unfinished statues, never releasing our talents and the abilities locked within. Our God-called possibilities lie deep within us, struggling to be liberated. We can set them free if we keep persevering and allow God to live through us.

A MATTER OF PERSPECTIVE

Life is fulfilling if you keep these points in mind:

- Love God and people—the two greatest commandments.
- Be thankful for all things. This "sweetener" makes life taste wonderful.
- Enjoy living. Stop and smell the roses. God made them for that reason.
- Don't quit. There's a prize waiting for you at the finish line.

I hope that you now understand that God doesn't intend your life on earth to be a pain, but a privilege. Not a worry, but a wonder. Not an obstacle, but an Opportunity.

Yes, life is truly wonderful. It's just a matter of how you view it.

MAKING THE MOST OF YOUR OPPORTUNITY

- Make sure that your motivation for serving God comes from love, not legalism.
- Write down the things that you are thankful for. During your prayer time each day, thank God for each item on your list.
- Start looking at circumstances from God's point of view.

THE RIDDLE

We're at the end of our time together. Hopefully, you have gained a new outlook on life. It has been my pleasure to share these thoughts with you.

But before we part company, let me pose for you a riddle: What is the most important thing that you can do with your life?

Advance your career? Collect the most toys? Or is it something spiritual like evangelism, prayer, or Bible memorization? Is it spending more time with your family? With so many things to do, it's hard to know which is the most important thing.

Here's the answer to the riddle: The most important thing you can do is *whatever God wants you to do at that moment.*

That might be throwing the ball to your son in your backyard. It might be working diligently at your job in the factory, washing the dishes, or feeding your newborn baby. It might be teaching Sunday school or serving in a ministry. It might be taking your wife out to dinner or your family on a vacation. If loving others is the second greatest commandment, then investing in your family certainly ought to be high on your priority list.

There are times when God wants us to pray and times when He wants us to play. Sometimes it is His will for us to give, and other times He wants us to get. At times He wants us to work, and other times He wants us to rest. "There is an appointed time for everything. And there is a time for every event under heaven" (Ecclesiastes 3:1).

It doesn't take huge accomplishments to make God smile. Now that you understand the meaning of your earthly existence, you can please Him even in the smallest matters of everyday life. Every day is now a new adventure, with each moment filled with wonder and purpose.

My prayer is that you will tell everyone about God's wonderful plan for eternity through Jesus Christ. Bring as many people as you can with you into God's heavenly kingdom.

It's time to lay down this book so you can start writing the remaining chapters of your life. You get to choose your own ending to your Opportunity. Make it a good one.

And don't forget to look me up when we get to the other side.

Multnomah Publishers®

The publisher and author would love to hear your comments about this book. *Please contact us at:*
www.multnomah.net/makingtodaycount

New Testament
Verses Pertaining to Eternity

Perhaps you have wondered where to find verses in the Bible that refer to eternity. Here are some New Testament Scriptures that pertain to the next life. If you spend some time reading through them, I think you will find them enlightening.

Matthew

5:11–12   "Blessed are you when people insult you and persecute you, and falsely say all kinds of evil against you because of Me. Rejoice and be glad, for your reward in heaven is great; for in the same way they persecuted the prophets who were before you."

5:19   "Whoever then annuls one of the least of these commandments, and teaches others to do the same, shall be called least in the kingdom of heaven; but whoever keeps and teaches them, he shall be called great in the kingdom of heaven."

5:22   "I say to you that everyone who is angry with his brother shall be guilty before the court; and whoever says to his brother, 'You good-for-nothing,' shall be guilty before the supreme court; and whoever says, 'You fool,' shall be guilty enough to go into the fiery hell."

5:29–30   "If your right eye makes you stumble, tear it out and throw it from you; for it is better for you to lose one of the parts of your body, than for your whole body to be thrown into hell. If your right hand makes you stumble, cut it off and throw it from you; for it is better for you to lose one of the parts of your body, than for your whole body to go into hell."

6:3–4   "When you give to the poor, do not let your left hand know what your right hand is doing, so that your giving will be in secret; and your Father who sees what is done in secret will reward you."

6:6   "When you pray, go into your inner room, close your door and pray to your Father who is in secret, and your Father who sees what is done in secret will reward you."

6:17–18   "When you fast, anoint your head and wash your face so that your fasting will not be noticed by men, but by your Father who is in secret; and your Father who sees what is done in secret will reward you."

6:20   "Store up for yourselves treasures in heaven, where neither moth nor rust destroys, and where thieves do not break in or steal."

7:13–14   "Enter through the narrow gate; for the gate is wide and the way is broad that leads to destruction, and there are many who enter through it. For the gate is small and the way is narrow that leads to life, and there are few who find it."

7:21   "Not everyone who says to Me, 'Lord, Lord,' will enter the kingdom of heaven, but he who does the will of My Father who is in heaven will enter."

8:11–12   "I say to you that many will come from east and west, and recline at the table with Abraham, Isaac and Jacob in the kingdom of heaven; but the sons of the kingdom will be cast out into the outer darkness; in that place there will be weeping and gnashing of teeth."

10:28   "Do not fear those who kill the body but are unable to kill the soul; but rather fear Him who is able to destroy both soul and body in hell."

10:41–42   "He who receives a prophet in the name of a prophet shall receive a prophet's reward; and he who receives a righteous man in the name of a righteous man shall receive a righteous man's reward. And whoever in the name of a disciple gives to one of these little ones even a cup of cold water to drink, truly I say to you, he shall not lose his reward."

11:21–24   "Woe to you, Chorazin! Woe to you, Bethsaida! For if the miracles had occurred in Tyre and Sidon which occurred in you, they would have repented long ago in sackcloth and ashes. Nevertheless I say to you, it will be more tolerable for Tyre and Sidon in the day of judgment than for you. And you, Capernaum, will not be exalted to heaven, will you? You will descend to Hades; for if the miracles had occurred in Sodom which occurred in you, it would have remained to this day. Nevertheless I say to you that it will be more tolerable for the land of Sodom in the day of judgment, than for you."

12:36–37   "I tell you that every careless word that people speak, they shall give an accounting for it in the day of judgment. For by your words you will be justified, and by your words you will be condemned."

12:41–42 "The men of Nineveh will stand up with this generation at the judgment, and will condemn it because they repented at the preaching of Jonah; and behold, something greater than Jonah is here. The Queen of the South will rise up with this generation at the judgment and will condemn it, because she came from the ends of the earth to hear the wisdom of Solomon; and behold, something greater than Solomon is here."

13:41–43 "The Son of Man will send forth His angels, and they will gather out of His kingdom all stumbling blocks, and those who commit lawlessness, and will throw them into the furnace of fire; in that place there will be weeping and gnashing of teeth. Then THE RIGHTEOUS WILL SHINE FORTH AS THE SUN in the kingdom of their Father. He who has ears, let him hear."

13:49–50 "So it will be at the end of the age; the angels will come forth and take out the wicked from among the righteous, and will throw them into the furnace of fire; in that place there will be weeping and gnashing of teeth."

16:25–27 "Whoever wishes to save his life will lose it; but whoever loses his life for My sake will find it. For what will it profit a man if he gains the whole world and forfeits his soul? Or what will a man give in exchange for his soul? For the Son of Man is going to come in the glory of His Father with His angels, and WILL THEN REPAY EVERY MAN ACCORDING TO HIS DEEDS."

18:4	"Whoever then humbles himself as this child, he is the greatest in the kingdom of heaven."
18:8–9	"If your hand or your foot causes you to stumble, cut it off and throw it from you; it is better for you to enter life crippled or lame, than to have two hands or two feet and be cast into the eternal fire. If your eye causes you to stumble, pluck it out and throw it from you. It is better for you to enter life with one eye, than to have two eyes and be cast into the fiery hell."
19:21	Jesus said to him, "If you wish to be complete, go and sell your possessions and give to the poor, and you will have treasure in heaven; and come, follow Me."
19:29–30	"Everyone who has left houses or brothers or sisters or father or mother or children or farms for My name's sake, will receive many times as much, and will inherit eternal life. But many who are first will be last; and the last, first."
20:26–27	"Whoever wishes to become great among you shall be your servant, and whoever wishes to be first among you shall be your slave."
22:13	"Then the king said to the servants, 'Bind him hand and foot, and throw him into the outer darkness; in that place there will be weeping and gnashing of teeth.'"
22:30	"In the resurrection [people] neither marry nor are given in marriage, but are like angels in heaven."
25:21	"His master said to him, 'Well done, good and faithful slave. You were faithful with a few things, I will put you in charge of many things; enter into the joy of your master.'"

25:30	"Throw out the worthless slave into the outer darkness; in that place there will be weeping and gnashing of teeth."
25:41, 46	"Then He will also say to those on His left, 'Depart from Me, accursed ones, into the eternal fire which has been prepared for the devil and his angels.'... These will go away into eternal punishment, but the righteous into eternal life."
26:29	"I say to you, I will not drink of this fruit of the vine from now on until that day when I drink it new with you in My Father's kingdom."

MARK

8:35–36	"Whoever wishes to save his life will lose it, but whoever loses his life for My sake and the gospel's will save it. For what does it profit a man to gain the whole world, and forfeit his soul?"
9:35	Sitting down, He called the twelve and said to them, "If anyone wants to be first, he shall be last of all and servant of all."
9:41	"Whoever gives you a cup of water to drink because of your name as followers of Christ, truly I say to you, he will not lose his reward."
9:43–48	"If your hand causes you to stumble, cut it off; it is better for you to enter life crippled, than, having your two hands, to go into hell, into the unquenchable fire, [where THEIR WORM DOES NOT DIE, AND THE FIRE IS NOT QUENCHED.] If your foot causes you to stumble, cut it off; it is better for you to enter life lame, than, having your two feet, to be cast into hell, [where THEIR WORM

DOES NOT DIE, AND THE FIRE IS NOT QUENCHED.]
If your eye causes you to stumble, throw it out; it is better for you to enter the kingdom of God with one eye, than, having two eyes, to be cast into hell, where THEIR WORM DOES NOT DIE, AND THE FIRE IS NOT QUENCHED."

10:21   Looking at him, Jesus felt a love for him and said to him, "One thing you lack: go and sell all you possess and give to the poor, and you will have treasure in heaven; and come, follow Me."

10:40   "To sit on My right or on My left, this is not Mine to give; but it is for those for whom it has been prepared."

10:42–44   Calling them to Himself, Jesus said to them, "You know that those who are recognized as rulers of the Gentiles lord it over them; and their great men exercise authority over them. But it is not this way among you, but whoever wishes to become great among you shall be your servant; and whoever wishes to be first among you shall be slave of all."

LUKE

1:33   "He will reign over the house of Jacob forever, and His kingdom will have no end."

6:22–23   "Blessed are you when men hate you, and ostracize you, and insult you, and scorn your name as evil, for the sake of the Son of Man. Be glad in that day and leap for joy, for behold, your reward is great in heaven. For in the same way their fathers used to treat the prophets."

6:35   "Love your enemies, and do good, and lend, expecting nothing in return; and your reward will be great, and you will be sons of the Most High; for He Himself is kind to ungrateful and evil men."

9:24–25   "Whoever wishes to save his life will lose it, but whoever loses his life for My sake, he is the one who will save it. For what is a man profited if he gains the whole world, and loses or forfeits himself?"

10:20   "Do not rejoice in this, that the spirits are subject to you, but rejoice that your names are recorded in heaven."

12:2–5   "There is nothing covered up that will not be revealed, and hidden that will not be known. Accordingly, whatever you have said in the dark will be heard in the light, and what you have whispered in the inner rooms will be proclaimed upon the housetops. I say to you, My friends, do not be afraid of those who kill the body and after that have no more that they can do. But I will warn you whom to fear: fear the One who, after He has killed, has authority to cast into hell; yes, I tell you, fear Him!"

12:33   "Sell your possessions and give to charity; make yourselves money belts which do not wear out, an unfailing treasure in heaven, where no thief comes near nor moth destroys."

13:1–3   Now on the same occasion there were some present who reported to Him about the Galileans whose blood Pilate had mixed with their sacrifices. And Jesus said to them, "Do you suppose that these Galileans were greater sinners than all other Galileans because they suffered this fate? I tell you, no, but unless you repent, you will all likewise perish."

13:28–30   "In that place there will be weeping and gnashing of teeth when you see Abraham and Isaac and Jacob and all the prophets in the kingdom of God, but yourselves being thrown out. And they will come from east and west and from north and south, and will recline at the table in the kingdom of God. And behold, some are last who will be first and some are first who will be last."

14:11   "Everyone who exalts himself will be humbled, and he who humbles himself will be exalted."

14:13–14   "When you give a reception, invite the poor, the crippled, the lame, the blind, and you will be blessed, since they do not have the means to repay you; for you will be repaid at the resurrection of the righteous."

16:9   "I say to you, make friends for yourselves by means of the wealth of unrighteousness, so that when it fails, they will receive you into the eternal dwellings."

16:11   "If you have not been faithful in the use of unrighteous wealth, who will entrust the true riches to you?"

16:23   "In Hades he lifted up his eyes, being in torment, and saw Abraham far away and Lazarus in his bosom."

18:25 "It is easier for a camel to go through the eye of a needle than for a rich man to enter the kingdom of God."

18:29–30 He said to them, "Truly I say to you, there is no one who has left house or wife or brothers or parents or children, for the sake of the kingdom of God, who will not receive many times as much at this time and in the age to come, eternal life."

19:15, 17 "When he returned, after receiving the kingdom, he ordered that these slaves, to whom he had given the money, be called to him so that he might know what business they had done.... And he said to him, 'Well done, good slave, because you have been faithful in a very little thing, you are to be in authority over ten cities.'"

20:34–36 Jesus said to them, "The sons of this age marry and are given in marriage, but those who are considered worthy to attain to that age and the resurrection from the dead, neither marry nor are given in marriage; for they cannot even die anymore, because they are like angels, and are sons of God, being sons of the resurrection."

22:18 "I say to you, I will not drink of the fruit of the vine from now on until the kingdom of God comes."

JOHN

3:16 "For God so loved the world, that He gave His only begotten Son, that whoever believes in Him shall not perish, but have eternal life."

5:24 "Truly, truly, I say to you, he who hears My word, and believes Him who sent Me, has eternal life, and does not come into judgment, but has passed out of death into life."

5:28–29   "Do not marvel at this; for an hour is coming, in which all who are in the tombs will hear His voice, and will come forth; those who did the good deeds to a resurrection of life, those who committed the evil deeds to a resurrection of judgment."

6:40   "This is the will of My Father, that everyone who beholds the Son and believes in Him will have eternal life, and I Myself will raise him up on the last day."

10:27–28   "My sheep hear My voice, and I know them, and they follow Me; and I give eternal life to them, and they will never perish; and no one will snatch them out of My hand."

11:25–26   Jesus said to her, "I am the resurrection and the life; he who believes in Me will live even if he dies, and everyone who lives and believes in Me will never die. Do you believe this?"

12:25   "He who loves his life loses it, and he who hates his life in this world will keep it to life eternal."

14:2   "In My Father's house are many dwelling places; if it were not so, I would have told you; for I go to prepare a place for you."

14:6   Jesus said to him, "I am the way, and the truth, and the life; no one comes to the Father but through Me."

18:36   Jesus answered, "My kingdom is not of this world. If My kingdom were of this world, then My servants would be fighting so that I would not be handed over to the Jews; but as it is, My kingdom is not of this realm."

ACTS

2:21   "And it shall be that everyone who calls on the name of the Lord will be saved."

10:43   "Of Him all the prophets bear witness that through His name everyone who believes in Him receives forgiveness of sins."

24:15   There shall certainly be a resurrection of both the righteous and the wicked.

ROMANS

1:20   Since the creation of the world His invisible attributes, His eternal power and divine nature, have been clearly seen, being understood through what has been made, so that they are without excuse.

2:16   [There will come a] day when, according to my gospel, God will judge the secrets of men through Christ Jesus.

5:9–10   Much more then, having now been justified by His blood, we shall be saved from the wrath of God through Him. For if while we were enemies we were reconciled to God through the death of His Son, much more, having been reconciled, we shall be saved by His life.

6:23   The wages of sin is death, but the free gift of God is eternal life in Christ Jesus our Lord.

8:11   If the Spirit of Him who raised Jesus from the dead dwells in you, He who raised Christ Jesus from the dead will also give life to your mortal bodies through His Spirit who dwells in you.

8:16–18   The Spirit Himself testifies with our spirit that we are children of God, and if children, heirs also, heirs of God and fellow heirs with Christ, if indeed we suffer with Him so that we may also be glorified with Him. For I consider that the sufferings of this present time are not worthy to be compared with the glory that is to be revealed to us.

8:23   Not only this, but also we ourselves, having the first fruits of the Spirit, even we ourselves groan within ourselves, waiting eagerly for our adoption as sons, the redemption of our body.

10:9–11, 13   If you confess with your mouth Jesus as Lord, and believe in your heart that God raised Him from the dead, you will be saved; for with the heart a person believes, resulting in righteousness, and with the mouth he confesses, resulting in salvation. For the Scripture says, "WHOEVER BELIEVES IN HIM WILL NOT BE DISAPPOINTED."… [and] "WHOEVER WILL CALL ON THE NAME OF THE LORD WILL BE SAVED."

14:10, 12   But you, why do you judge your brother? Or you again, why do you regard your brother with contempt? For we will all stand before the judgment seat of God.… So then each one of us will give an account of himself to God.

1 CORINTHIANS

3:8   He who plants and he who waters are one; but each will receive his own reward according to his own labor.

3:12–15   If any man builds on the foundation with gold, silver, precious stones, wood, hay, straw, each man's
work will become evident; for the day will show it
because it is to be revealed with fire, and the fire
itself will test the quality of each man's work. If
any man's work which he has built on it remains,
he will receive a reward. If any man's work is
burned up, he will suffer loss; but he himself will
be saved, yet so as through fire.

4:5   Do not go on passing judgment before the time,
but wait until the Lord comes who will both bring
to light the things hidden in the darkness and dis-
close the motives of men's hearts; and then each
man's praise will come to him from God.

6:2–3   Do you not know that the saints will judge the
world? If the world is judged by you, are you not
competent to constitute the smallest law courts?
Do you not know that we will judge angels? How
much more matters of this life?

6:9–11   Do you not know that the unrighteous will not
inherit the kingdom of God? Do not be deceived;
neither fornicators, nor idolaters, nor adulterers, nor
effeminate, nor homosexuals, nor thieves, nor the
covetous, nor drunkards, nor revilers, nor
swindlers, will inherit the kingdom of God. Such
were some of you; but you were washed, but you
were sanctified, but you were justified in the name
of the Lord Jesus Christ and in the Spirit of our God.

9:17   If I do this voluntarily, I have a reward; but if against
my will, I have a stewardship entrusted to me.

9:24–25   Do you not know that those who run in a race all run, but only one receives the prize? Run in such a way that you may win. Everyone who competes in the games exercises self-control in all things. They then do it to receive a perishable wreath, but we an imperishable.

13:12   Now we see in a mirror dimly, but then face to face; now I know in part, but then I will know fully just as I also have been fully known.

15:41–44   There is one glory of the sun, and another glory of the moon, and another glory of the stars; for star differs from star in glory. So also is the resurrection of the dead. It is sown a perishable body, it is raised an imperishable body; it is sown in dishonor, it is raised in glory; it is sown in weakness, it is raised in power; it is sown a natural body, it is raised a spiritual body. If there is a natural body, there is also a spiritual body.

15:49, 51–52   Just as we have borne the image of the earthy, we will also bear the image of the heavenly.… We will all be changed, in a moment, in the twinkling of an eye, at the last trumpet; for the trumpet will sound, and the dead will be raised imperishable, and we will be changed.

15:58   Therefore, my beloved brethren, be steadfast, immovable, always abounding in the work of the Lord, knowing that your toil is not in vain in the Lord.

2 CORINTHIANS

4:17–18   Momentary, light affliction is producing for us an eternal weight of glory far beyond all comparison,

while we look not at the things which are seen,
but at the things which are not seen; for the things
which are seen are temporal, but the things which
are not seen are eternal.

5:1   We know that if the earthly tent which is our house
is torn down, we have a building from God, a
house not made with hands, eternal in the heavens.

5:10   We must all appear before the judgment seat of
Christ, so that each one may be recompensed for
his deeds in the body, according to what he has
done, whether good or bad.

GALATIANS

6:7–8   Do not be deceived, God is not mocked; for whatever a man sows, this he will also reap. For the
one who sows to his own flesh will from the flesh
reap corruption, but the one who sows to the
Spirit will from the Spirit reap eternal life.

EPHESIANS

2:6–9   [God] raised us up with Him, and seated us with
Him in the heavenly places in Christ Jesus, so that
in the ages to come He might show the surpassing
riches of His grace in kindness toward us in Christ
Jesus. For by grace you have been saved through
faith; and that not of yourselves, it is the gift of
God; not as a result of works, so that no one may
boast.

5:5   For this you know with certainty, that no immoral
or impure person or covetous man, who is an
idolater, has an inheritance in the kingdom of
Christ and God.

6:5–9   Slaves, be obedient to those who are your masters according to the flesh, with fear and trembling, in the sincerity of your heart, as to Christ; not by way of eyeservice, as men-pleasers, but as slaves of Christ, doing the will of God from the heart. With good will render service, as to the Lord, and not to men, knowing that whatever good thing each one does, this he will receive back from the Lord, whether slave or free. And masters, do the same things to them, and give up threatening, knowing that both their Master and yours is in heaven, and there is no partiality with Him.

PHILIPPIANS

1:23   I am hard-pressed from both directions, having the desire to depart and be with Christ, for that is very much better.

3:20   Our citizenship is in heaven, from which also we eagerly wait for a Savior, the Lord Jesus Christ.

COLOSSIANS

1:13   He rescued us from the domain of darkness, and transferred us to the kingdom of His beloved Son.

3:1–2   If you have been raised up with Christ, keep seeking the things above, where Christ is, seated at the right hand of God. Set your mind on the things above, not on the things that are on earth.

3:23–25   Whatever you do, do your work heartily, as for the Lord rather than for men, knowing that from the Lord you will receive the reward of the inheritance. It is the Lord Christ whom you serve. For he who does wrong will receive the consequences of the wrong which he has done, and that without partiality.

1 THESSALONIANS

2:12   Walk in a manner worthy of the God who calls you into His own kingdom and glory.

4:16–17   The Lord Himself will descend from heaven with a shout, with the voice of the archangel and with the trumpet of God, and the dead in Christ will rise first. Then we who are alive and remain will be caught up together with them in the clouds to meet the Lord in the air, and so we shall always be with the Lord.

5:9   God has not destined us for wrath, but for obtaining salvation through our Lord Jesus Christ.

2 THESSALONIANS

1:6–9   It is only just for God to repay with affliction those who afflict you, and to give relief to you who are afflicted and to us as well when the Lord Jesus will be revealed from heaven with His mighty angels in flaming fire, dealing out retribution to those who do not know God and to those who do not obey the gospel of our Lord Jesus. These will pay the penalty of eternal destruction, away from the presence of the Lord and from the glory of His power.

2:16–17   May our Lord Jesus Christ Himself and God our Father, who has loved us and given us eternal comfort and good hope by grace, comfort and strengthen your hearts in every good work and word.

I TIMOTHY

2:3–4   This is good and acceptable in the sight of God our Savior, who desires all men to be saved and to come to the knowledge of the truth.

6:7   We have brought nothing into the world, so we cannot take anything out of it either.

6:17–19   Instruct those who are rich in this present world not to be conceited or to fix their hope on the uncertainty of riches, but on God, who richly supplies us with all things to enjoy. Instruct them to do good, to be rich in good works, to be generous and ready to share, storing up for themselves the treasure of a good foundation for the future, so that they may take hold of that which is life indeed.

2 TIMOTHY

1:9   [God] has saved us and called us with a holy calling, not according to our works, but according to His own purpose and grace which was granted us in Christ Jesus from all eternity.

4:1   I solemnly charge you in the presence of God and of Christ Jesus, who is to judge the living and the dead.

4:7–8   I have fought the good fight, I have finished the course, I have kept the faith; in the future there is laid up for me the crown of righteousness, which the Lord, the righteous Judge, will award to me on that day; and not only to me, but also to all who have loved His appearing.

4:14   Alexander the coppersmith did me much harm;
            the Lord will repay him according to his deeds.

4:18   The Lord will rescue me from every evil deed, and
            will bring me safely to His heavenly kingdom; to
            Him be the glory forever and ever. Amen.

TITUS

3:5   He saved us, not on the basis of deeds which we
            have done in righteousness, but according to His
            mercy, by the washing of regeneration and renew-
            ing by the Holy Spirit.

HEBREWS

6:10   God is not unjust so as to forget your work and the
            love which you have shown toward His name, in
            having ministered and in still ministering to the
            saints.

9:27   It is appointed for men to die once and after this
            comes judgment.

10:34   You showed sympathy to the prisoners and
            accepted joyfully the seizure of your property,
            knowing that you have for yourselves a better pos-
            session and a lasting one.

11:10   He was looking for the city which has founda-
            tions, whose architect and builder is God.

11:16   They desire a better country, that is, a heavenly
            one. Therefore God is not ashamed to be called
            their God; for He has prepared a city for them.

11:26   [Moses considered] the reproach of Christ greater
            riches than the treasures of Egypt; for he was look-
            ing to the reward.

12:22   You have come to Mount Zion and to the city of the living God, the heavenly Jerusalem, and to myriads of angels.

12:28   Therefore, since we receive a kingdom which cannot be shaken, let us show gratitude, by which we may offer to God an acceptable service with reverence and awe.

13:14   Here we do not have a lasting city, but we are seeking the city which is to come.

JAMES

1:12   Blessed is a man who perseveres under trial; for once he has been approved, he will receive the crown of life which the Lord has promised to those who love Him.

2:5   Listen, my beloved brethren: did not God choose the poor of this world to be rich in faith and heirs of the kingdom which He promised to those who love Him?

2:13   Judgment will be merciless to one who has shown no mercy; mercy triumphs over judgment.

4:10   Humble yourselves in the presence of the Lord, and He will exalt you.

4:14   You are just a vapor that appears for a little while and then vanishes away.

5:9   Do not complain, brethren, against one another, so that you yourselves may not be judged; behold, the Judge is standing right at the door.

5:12   Above all, my brethren, do not swear, either by heaven or by earth or with any other oath; but your yes is to be yes, and your no, no, so that you may not fall under judgment.

1 PETER

1:3–4   Blessed be the God and Father of our Lord Jesus Christ, who according to His great mercy has caused us to be born again to a living hope through the resurrection of Jesus Christ from the dead, to obtain an inheritance which is imperishable and undefiled and will not fade away, reserved in heaven for you.

1:17   If you address as Father the One who impartially judges according to each one's work, conduct yourselves in fear during the time of your stay on earth.

3:8–9   All of you be harmonious, sympathetic, brotherly, kindhearted, and humble in spirit; not returning evil for evil or insult for insult, but giving a blessing instead; for you were called for the very purpose that you might inherit a blessing.

4:5   [Gentiles] will give account to Him who is ready to judge the living and the dead.

4:13, 17   To the degree that you share the sufferings of Christ, keep on rejoicing, so that also at the revelation of His glory you may rejoice with exultation.... For it is time for judgment to begin with the household of God; and if it begins with us first, what will be the outcome for those who do not obey the gospel of God?

5:4   And when the Chief Shepherd appears, you will receive the unfading crown of glory.

5:5–6

You younger men, likewise, be subject to your elders; and all of you, clothe yourselves with humility toward one another, for GOD IS OPPOSED TO THE PROUD, BUT GIVES GRACE TO THE HUMBLE. Therefore humble yourselves under the mighty hand of God, that He may exalt you at the proper time.

2 PETER

1:10–11

Therefore, brethren, be all the more diligent to make certain about His calling and choosing you; for as long as you practice these things, you will never stumble; for in this way the entrance into the eternal kingdom of our Lord and Savior Jesus Christ will be abundantly supplied to you.

2:4, 9

If God did not spare angels when they sinned, but cast them into hell and committed them to pits of darkness, reserved for judgment…then the Lord knows how to rescue the godly from temptation, and to keep the unrighteous under punishment for the day of judgment.

3:7

By His word the present heavens and earth are being reserved for fire, kept for the day of judgment and destruction of ungodly men.

3:10–13

The day of the Lord will come like a thief, in which the heavens will pass away with a roar and the elements will be destroyed with intense heat, and the earth and its works will be burned up. Since all these things are to be destroyed in this way, what sort of people ought you to be in holy conduct and godliness, looking for and hastening the coming of the day of God, because of which the heavens will be destroyed by burning, and the elements will melt with intense heat! But according to His promise we are looking for new heavens and a new earth, in which righteousness dwells.

1 John

2:17 The world is passing away, and also its lusts; but the one who does the will of God lives forever.

4:17 By this, love is perfected with us, so that we may have confidence in the day of judgment; because as He is, so also are we in this world.

5:13 These things I have written to you who believe in the name of the Son of God, so that you may know that you have eternal life.

2 John

1:8 Watch yourselves, that you do not lose what we have accomplished, but that you may receive a full reward.

Jude

1:6–7 Angels who did not keep their own domain, but abandoned their proper abode, He has kept in eternal bonds under darkness for the judgment of the great day, just as Sodom and Gomorrah and the cities around them, since they in the same way as these indulged in gross immorality and went after strange flesh, are exhibited as an example in undergoing the punishment of eternal fire.

REVELATION

1:6   He has made us to be a kingdom, priests to His God and Father—to Him be the glory and the dominion forever and ever. Amen.

2:7   "He who has an ear, let him hear what the Spirit says to the churches. To him who overcomes, I will grant to eat of the tree of life which is in the Paradise of God."

2:10–11   "Do not fear what you are about to suffer. Behold, the devil is about to cast some of you into prison, so that you will be tested, and you will have tribulation for ten days. Be faithful until death, and I will give you the crown of life. He who has an ear, let him hear what the Spirit says to the churches. He who overcomes will not be hurt by the second death."

2:17   "He who has an ear, let him hear what the Spirit says to the churches. To him who overcomes, to him I will give some of the hidden manna, and I will give him a white stone, and a new name written on the stone which no one knows but he who receives it."

2:26   "He who overcomes, and he who keeps My deeds until the end, TO HIM I WILL GIVE AUTHORITY OVER THE NATIONS."

3:5   "He who overcomes will thus be clothed in white garments; and I will not erase his name from the book of life, and I will confess his name before My Father and before His angels."

3:11–12   "I am coming quickly; hold fast what you have, so that no one will take your crown. He who overcomes, I will make him a pillar in the temple of

My God, and he will not go out from it anymore; and I will write on him the name of My God, and the name of the city of My God, the new Jerusalem, which comes down out of heaven from My God, and My new name."

3:21   "He who overcomes, I will grant to him to sit down with Me on My throne, as I also overcame and sat down with My Father on His throne."

21:1–4   I saw a new heaven and a new earth; for the first heaven and the first earth passed away, and there is no longer any sea. And I saw the holy city, new Jerusalem, coming down out of heaven from God, made ready as a bride adorned for her husband. And I heard a loud voice from the throne, saying, "Behold, the tabernacle of God is among men, and He will dwell among them, and they shall be His people, and God Himself will be among them, and He will wipe away every tear from their eyes; and there will no longer be any death; there will no longer be any mourning, or crying, or pain; the first things have passed away."

21:16, 21   The city is laid out as a square, and its length is as great as the width; and he measured the city with the rod, fifteen hundred miles; its length and width and height are equal.... And the twelve gates were twelve pearls; each one of the gates was a single pearl. And the street of the city was pure gold, like transparent glass.

21:23–27   The city has no need of the sun or of the moon to shine on it, for the glory of God has illumined it, and its lamp is the Lamb. The nations will walk by its light, and the kings of the earth will bring their glory into it. In the daytime (for there will be no night there) its gates will never be closed; and they will bring the glory and the honor of the nations into it; and nothing unclean, and no one who practices abomination and lying, shall ever come into it, but only those whose names are written in the Lamb's book of life.

22:1–5   Then he showed me a river of the water of life, clear as crystal, coming from the throne of God and of the Lamb, in the middle of its street. On either side of the river was the tree of life, bearing twelve kinds of fruit, yielding its fruit every month; and the leaves of the tree were for the healing of the nations. There will no longer be any curse; and the throne of God and of the Lamb will be in it, and His bond-servants will serve Him; they will see His face, and His name will be on their foreheads. And there will no longer be any night; and they will not have need of the light of a lamp nor the light of the sun, because the Lord God will illumine them; and they will reign forever and ever.

NOTES

CHAPTER TWO

1. Greg Potts, *Proclaim* (July/September 1993).
2. *The Hymnbook* (Philadelphia: John Ribble, 1950), 12.

CHAPTER FOUR

1. Norval Geldenhuys, *The New International Commentary on the New Testament: Commentary on the Gospel of Luke* (Grand Rapids, Mich.: Wm. B. Eerdmans Publishing Company, 1977), 475.
2. Elsa Rand, *Introduction to Prophecy* (Findlay, Ohio: Dunham, 1960), 228.

CHAPTER FIVE

1. Kent Hughes, *Pastor to Pastor*, Focus on the Family taped interview, vol. 13 (1994).
2. Charles Haddon Spurgeon, *The Gospel of Matthew* (Grand Rapids, Mich.: Fleming H. Revell, 1987), 365.

CHAPTER SIX

1. *Leadership* (spring 1995), 49.
2. Corrie ten Boom, *The Hiding Place* (New York: Bantam Books, 1971), 238.
3. Rick Ezell, *Ministry on the Cutting Edge* (Grand Rapids, Mich.: Kregel, 1995), 80.
4. *Daily Bread* (Grand Rapids, Mich.: RBC Ministries, 5 September 1995).

CHAPTER SEVEN

1. Rick Howard, *The Judgment Seat of Christ* (Woodside, Calif.: Naioth Sound and Publishing, 1990), 6–7.
2. Ibid., 34.
3. Gerhard Gschwandtner, "Lies and Deceptions in Selling," in *Personal Selling Power* (May/June 1992), 63.

CHAPTER EIGHT

1. *Bits & Pieces* (4 February 1993), 24.
2. Roland Leavell, *Studies in Matthew* (Nashville, Tenn.: Convention Press, 1962), 115.
3. John Walvoord, *The Revelation of Jesus Christ* (Chicago, Ill.: Moody Press, 1966), 330.

CHAPTER NINE

1. Erwin Lutzer, *One Minute after You Die* (Chicago, Ill.: Moody Press, 1997), 88–9.
2. John Walvoord, *The Revelation of Jesus Christ* (Chicago, Ill.: Moody Press, 1966), 171.

CHAPTER TEN

1. From *Leadership* by Sandy Reynolds, as cited in Raymond McHenry, *The Best of In Other Words* (1996), 135.
2. Walter Knight, *Knight's Master Book of New Illustrations* (Grand Rapids, Mich.: Wm. B. Eerdmans Publishing Company, 1956), 315.
3. Brian Harbour, *Brian's Lines* (November 1989).

CHAPTER TWELVE

1. Robert Hastings, *Proclaim* (January/March, 1993), 28.

CHAPTER THIRTEEN

1. Kirk Douglas, *The Ragman's Son* (New York: Pocket Books, 1988), 420.